Women have needs which men do not understand. Here are workable solutions to the problems and frustrations today's woman faces in her home and family life. She can break the shackles of emotional isolation, discover greater self-esteem and acceptance, and describe her *real* need for romantic love. This book shows the way to find satisfying solutions.

What wives wish their husbands knew about women

Dr. James Dobson

LIVING BOOKS
Tyndale House Publishers, Inc.
Wheaton, Illinois

Eleventh printing, Living Books edition, April 1983

Library of Congress Catalog Card Number 75-15029
ISBN 8423-7890-1, cloth
ISBN 8423-7889-8, paper
ISBN 8423-7896-0 Living Books edition

To a little fellow named Ryan,
who loves caterpillars and hates baths
and tolerates girls
and can ask a million questions an hour
("Mom, do worms yawn?"),
I affectionately dedicate this book
and pledge my very best efforts
as his loving father.

Contents

CHAPTER ONE

Mom: The Domestic Engineer

You may have noticed that this book is dedicated to my beloved son, Ryan. This little lad is now three years old, and he is a certified, card-carrying toddler. He has *every* single characteristic described in the textbooks as being typical for children between eighteen and forty months of age. During this dynamic period of life, emotional enthusiasm and excitement are supposed to bubble forth from some inexhaustible wellspring of energy, and so it has been with Ryan. In fact, *the* very day he turned eighteen months of age, it was as though a little voice whispered in his ear, "Now, kid, now!" Ryan began running that afternoon and he's still moving at maximum velocity. He isn't a malicious child and he rarely defies authority in a blatant manner. But he is enormously curious and he gets into everything. If it is humanly possible, Ryan can be expected to spill it, break it, disassemble it, spread it, or render it inoperable. Trying to get him to be still and quiet is like nailing jello to a tree: it's impossible! And, of course, his personal safety teeters on the brink of disaster from moment to moment. In fact, it is necessary for an emotionally stable adult to follow Ryan around all day, just to keep him from killing himself! Occasionally that responsibility falls to me.

I was at home alone with Ryan one morning when I suddenly realized that it had been approximately two minutes since my little explorer had made any noise. (When one baby-sits with Ryan, silence is definitely *not* golden.) I immediately began looking for him, searching each room of the house, but he was not to be found. Finally, I glanced through the kitchen window and saw that Ryan had managed to crawl into the back of a truck which some builders had parked in our driveway. The bed of the truck was taller than Ryan's head, and it is still a mystery as to how he climbed so high. When I found him, he was trying desperately to get down. He was hanging off the back of the truck from his waist downward, yet his feet were still suspended twelve to fifteen inches above the ground. Seeing that he was going to fall, I slipped up behind him without him hearing me coming and placed my hands outward to catch him when he fell. But as I drew nearer, I heard him talking to himself. He was not crying. He didn't complain or scream in terror. He was simply probing empty space with one foot and saying softly, "Somebody help the boy! Won't somebody come help the boy?" His words characterized his way of life, for "helping the boy" has become a full-time job for Ryan's loving mother and me.

Shortly after the truck-bed experience, little Ryan let me see another side of his sparkling personality. My wife, Shirley, broke her leg while skiing, thereby granting me the chance to do *her* thing for a few weeks. I learned a great deal during that time about the color of grass on the other side of the fence: it not only wasn't any greener . . . it wasn't even edible! The very first morning that I was on the job, Ryan began teaching me the rules to the game called motherhood. He awakened me with a loud cry at 6 A.M. Being jarred from a deep, dreamy sleep, I staggered from my bed and began feeling my way across the house toward Ryan's room. All this time he was crying at the top of his lungs. (That sound has much the same effect on the nerves as fingernails scratching a chalkboard.) When I reached his door and pushed it open, the crying suddenly stopped and a cheery little voice said, "Is breakfast ready?" I said, "I'm doing the best I can, Ryan!"

So I went into the kitchen to fix the kid something palatable to eat, but was still at least 80 percent asleep. I stood there staring into the cabinets with unfocused eyes, hoping something quick and simple would tumble out. Meanwhile, Ryan had climbed down from his bed and followed me into the kitchen. He tried repeatedly to engage me in conversation—which was the last thing on earth that his sleepy father wanted or needed at that moment.

He was saying, "Are we having bacon?"
and "Why isn't the milk poured?"
and "Is it almost ready?"
But I was ignoring his inquiries. He must have asked me a dozen questions, all of which went unanswered. Then I "tuned in" just in time to hear him sigh and say, "I'm getting so tired of you!"

So what's a mother to do, folks? I don't know! I went back and reread my book *Dare to Discipline* but it didn't say anything about handling the pre-sunrise activities of an ambitious toddler. I told my wife if she would just come back to work I would rise up and call her blessed each day, as I sit among the elders in the gates.[1] In fact, I could hardly wait to sit among the elders in the gates again.

Through these brief forays into the responsibilities of motherhood and from the experience gained in counseling women, I have developed a deep appreciation for the unique skills required of wives and mothers. In my view, their job is of utmost importance to the health and vitality of our society, and I regret the lack of respect and status given to today's "housewives." Even that word "housewife" has come to symbolize unfulfillment, inferiority, and insignificance. How unfortunate! We can make no greater mistake as a nation than to devalue the importance of the home and the sustenance which children should be given there.

However, "home-work" imposes some special frustrations and tensions on women, and we should face them squarely. Even for a mother who is deeply committed to her family and its welfare, there may be times when she feels like running away from her tribe. Small children, such as Ryan, can be exhausting and irritating to those who must care for them 365 days per year. The little butterballs are noisy and they bicker with each other and they make incredible messes and they wet their pants and they scratch the furniture and they steadily unravel mom's jangled nerves throughout the long days. Truly, it takes a superwoman to raise a bevy of children without occasionally wondering, "What in the world am I doing here?!"

Women also encounter other problems and pressures which are less common among men. Loneliness for adult companionship is particularly prevalent for the woman who remains at home. She often experiences deep, persistent yearnings for human contact. She longs for laughter and love and the romantic moments from her own younger days. Her daily dedication to soap operas on television is a reflection of this need for involvement in the lives of people, for her existence has become so isolated. It is no small problem.

This brings us to the most common source of frustration expressed to me in marital counseling: women who have experienced the unmet needs described above are often totally incapable of explaining their feelings to their husbands. The wife who knows something vital has disappeared from her life naturally reaches out to her man to supply the missing ingredient. She desperately wants him to understand her fears and frustrations, but she can't seem to get through to him. Oh, she tries, no doubt about that! But instead of her effort bringing empathy and support, it is likely to be interpreted as nagging, complaining, self-pity, and eye-gouging hostility of various forms. And every man alive is equipped with a little button somewhere in the center of his skull which permits him to "tune out" that kind of unnecessary noise. One wife wrote me the following note, expressing the precise sentiments of a million others: "Lack of communication causes most of my depression. When I try to resolve our problems or talk about them, my husband gives me a cold wall of silence. He becomes extremely negative whenever I try to discuss anything. He feels we have no problems!"

Now I have not written this book to bad-rap American men. We've had plenty of that in recent years. It has become popular to depict father as an idiot, a bigot, an exploiter, a misogynist, a football fanatic, a sex-maniac, and a self-centered egotist. To hear some angry females tell it, men are lower than a snake on snowshoes. Being a man myself, I tend to take those charges rather personally. But it is true, I believe, that too many men do not understand the emotional needs of their wives. They live in a vastly different world with ample frustrations of their own. Either they are unable to put themselves in a woman's place, seeing and feeling what she experiences, or else they are preoccupied with their own work and simply aren't listening. For whatever reason, women have needs which men do not comprehend. It is this breakdown of understanding that has motivated this book and its title, *What Wives Wish Their Husbands Knew About Women.*

The remaining pages of this text, then, are devoted to the American woman, with particular reference to her home and family life. There *are* workable solutions to the problems and frustrations which she faces there, and I have shared some of the approaches which have been effective in the lives of others. I have also discussed the nature of feminine emotions and how they influence her day-by-day activities. In short, the message of this book is designed to accomplish these objectives:

1. Help women explain their unique needs to their husbands.
2. Assist in breaking the shackles of emotional isolation.
3. Provide the keys to more fulfilling motherhood.
4. Discuss the common sources of depression in women, and their solutions.
5. Offer specific answers to everyday irritants.
6. Point the pathway toward greater self-esteem and acceptance.
7. Describe the *real* meaning of romantic love.

These are ambitious purposes, admittedly, and they sound a bit like the Preamble to the U.S. Constitution. However, it is easier to shoot straight when one knows where the target is. Let's begin with a discussion of the sources of depression in women.

CHAPTER TWO

Sources of Depression in Women

Perhaps the most inescapable conclusion I have drawn from psychological counseling of women concerns the commonness of depression and emotional apathy as a recurring fact of life. The majority of adult females seem to experience these times of despair, discouragement, disinterest, distress, despondency, and disenchantment with circumstances as they are. I have come to call this condition "The D's" for obvious reasons. A counselee will say, "I have the D's today," and I know precisely what she means.

Depression is not uniquely characteristic of women, certainly. But it occurs less frequently in men and is apparently more *crisis* oriented. In other words, men get depressed over specific problems such as a business setback or an illness. However, they are less likely to experience the vague, generalized, almost unidentifiable feeling of discouragement which many women encounter on a regular basis. Even a cloudy day may be enough to bring on a physical and emotional slowdown, known as the blahs, for those who are particularly vulnerable to depression.

The impact of depression can be minimized somewhat by an understanding of the cyclical nature of emotions occurring in both sexes. Haven't you observed from your own experience that highs are followed by lows and lows by highs? There is a regular fluctuation, almost like a mathematical sine curve (illustrated below) from a peak of enthusiasm to the depth of gloominess.

Furthermore, individual personalities do not extend much farther in one direction than they do the other. In other words, if we draw a line across the middle of the curve, symbolizing the emotional center (neither high nor low), the distance from there to the peak for a particular person, is almost the same as the distance from there to the valley. Let's look at an example or two: Type I people, characterized below, don't get very excited about anything. These Steady Freddies and Stable Mabels don't cheer enthusiastically at football games and their laughter is never boisterous. Good news is received about as calmly as bad. On the other hand, they never get very discouraged, either. They are rather dull people, but at least they're consistently dull! You can count on them. Today will be much like yesterday, tomorrow, and next November.

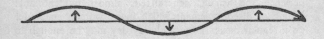

TYPE I PERSONALITIES

By contrast, Type II people (symbolized below) are the world's true "swingers." Their emotions bounce from the rafters down to the basement and back up the wall again.

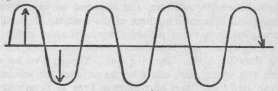

TYPE II PERSONALITIES

We all know at least one Type II individual who gets extremely happy every now and then. He arises in the morning and giggles at the very thought of the sunrise. He waves at the birds and grins at the flowers and whistles zippity-doo-dah throughout the day. Beware of this jolly fellow! I can guarantee you that he is going to crash not many days hence. And when he falls, great will be the collapse and disintegration thereof. Nothing will go right and life won't be worth living and he will have no friends and woe will fill the entire earth. He's so sentimental he will even weep at supermarket openings. He is, truly, an emotional yo-yo. And for reasons known only to a confused Cupid, this Type II extremist will probably marry a Type I bore, and the two of them will scratch and claw each other regularly for the next forty years.

My wife and I attended a symphony in Berlin during our first trip to Europe. Sitting in front of us was a young man who was probably studying music at a local university. He went into some kind of strange ecstasy during the first half of the performance, swaying to the orchestration with his eyes closed, and standing to cheer after every number. Following the last performance before the intermission, he went crazy with delight; you would have thought USC had just scored the winning touchdown against Notre Dame for the national championship. He yelled "Bravo! Bravo!" and waved to the conductor. But wouldn't you know, the second half of the performance made him sick. He slumped in his chair, booed the orchestra, and muttered his displeasure throughout the remaining hour of the concert. He finally sprang to his feet and pushed toward the aisle, stepping on toes, knees, and Beethoven's Fifth Symphony, stalking from the auditorium in a huff. Though I've never seen this young man, either before or after the concert, I can safely state that he typifies a Type II personality. His capacity for a "high," demonstrated in the first half of the performance, was matched by an equal and opposite "low" as the evening progressed. Frankly, I enjoyed his antics more than I did the music, but I wouldn't want him as a brother-in-law. He had more "hang-ups" than the phone company. Don't you know his wife has some interesting stories to tell . . . ?

It is also helpful to understand the nature of emotional rhythm in human beings. Anything producing an extreme "high" will set the stage for a later "low," and vice versa. About a year ago, for example, my wife and I bought a newer home. We had waited several years to find the right house, and we became very excited when escrow closed and the property was finally ours. The elation lasted for several days, during which time I discussed the experience with Shirley. I mentioned that we had been very high and that our excitement could not continue indefinitely. Emotions don't operate at maximum velocity for very long. More important, it was likely that our mental set would drop below sea level within a short period of time. As expected, we both experienced a vague letdown into mild depression about three days later. The house didn't seem so wonderful and there wasn't anything worth much enthusiasm. However, having anticipated the "downer," we recognized and accepted its temporary fluctuation when it came.

Your own depression will be more tolerable if you understand it as a relatively predictable occurrence. It is likely to appear, for instance, following a busy holiday, the birth of a baby, a job promotion, or even after a restful vacation. The cause for this phenomenon is partly physical in nature. Obviously, elation consumes greater quantities of body energy, since all systems are operating at an accelerated rate. The necessary consequence of this pace is fatigue and exhaustion, bringing with it a more depressed state. Thus, highs *must* be followed by lows. The system is governed by a psychological law. You can depend on it. But in the healthy individual, thank goodness, lows eventually give way to highs, too.

Returning to my earlier statement, it is not the "normal" fluctuation from high to low which causes me concern. Rather, it is the tendency of many women to remain in a depressed state much longer than should be expected. Instead of oscillating from high to low, these people may remain blue and discouraged for two or three weeks every month. Some are perpetually trapped in the emotional cellar for years without relief. The recurring presence of this complaint in my professional experience has led me to explore its causes and solutions.

Before difficult problems can be solved, they must be understood. For example, the guilty poliomyelitis virus had to be identified and isolated before Dr. Jonas Salk could produce a vaccine to combat it. In like manner, I set about identifying and isolating the specific causes for inordinate periods of depression in women. I had already observed in counseling sessions that the same frustrations and irritations were reflected by women of varying ages and backgrounds. There were, in fact, ten problems which had become extremely familiar to me. I had heard them repeated enough to have memorized the typical circumstances surrounding each irritation. Therefore, I devised a simple, ten-item questionnaire entitled "Sources of Depression in Women," on which are listed those recurring themes. Printed on the next page is a copy of that brief test.

Later, I asked approximately seventy-five women to rank the ten items appearing on the questionnaire according to their frustration from each source. The most depressing of the ten was to be given a 1; the least relevant item was scored 10. By averaging the results, it was then possible to determine which problems were most influential in the lives of the women surveyed.

While this study was never intended to meet the rigid specifications of the scientific method in every detail, it is interesting to know something about the women who completed the questionnaire. The seventy-five participants were married women between twenty-seven and forty years old; the mean age was probably about thirty-two. The majority were mothers who still had small children at home. Since the questionnaire was given in two church settings, most of the women professed to being dedicated to the Christian faith. They were predominately middle-class, suburban housewives. Each was asked to rank the items in privacy, not indicating her name or other personal identification. (This questionnaire has more recently been discussed with 5000 women participating in Family Life Seminars, verifying the validity of the original findings.)

The results of the questionnaire are presented on the following pages, with the ten sources of depression appearing in the order indicated by approximately half of the participants. (The rankings for the second group were very similar to the first, but were not identical.) Before reading further, however, it is suggested that the reader complete the questionnaire on his own behalf. Women should number a sheet of paper from 1 to 10, and then rank the items twice: The first time through, rank them according to your own experience; the second time, rank them as you think the other women probably did as a group. Male readers might want to do this second ranking, guessing the responses of the study group.

Sources of Depression Among Women

Please rank the following sources of depression according to their applicability in your life. Do not sign your name.

	IRRITANT	YOUR RANK	GUESSED RANK
1.	Absence of *romantic* love in my marriage.	____	____
2.	In-law conflict.	____	____
3.	Low self-esteem.	____	____
4.	Problems with the children.	____	____
5.	Financial difficulties.	____	____
6.	Loneliness, isolation, and boredom.	____	____
7.	Sexual problems in marriage.	____	____
8.	Menstrual and physiological problems.	____	____
9.	Fatigue and time pressure.	____	____
10.	Aging.	____	____

CHAPTER THREE

Low Self-Esteem

Believe it or not, *Low Self-Esteem* was indicated as *the* most troubling problem by the majority of the women completing the questionnaire. More than 50 percent of the group marked this item above every other alternative on the list, and 80 percent placed it in the top five. This finding is perfectly consistent with my own observations and expectations: even in seemingly healthy and happily married young women, personal inferiority and self-doubt cut the deepest and leave the most wicked scars. This same old nemesis is usually revealed within the first five minutes of a counseling session; feelings of inadequacy, lack of confidence, and a certainty of worthlessness have become a way of life, or too often, a way of despair for millions of American women.

What does it mean to have low self-esteem? What does one experience when struggling with deep-seated feelings of inadequacy? Perhaps I can express the troubling thoughts and anxieties which reverberate through the backroads of an insecure mind. It is sitting alone in a house during the quiet afternoon hours, wondering why the phone doesn't ring . . . wondering why you have no "real" friends. It is longing for someone to talk to, soul to soul, but knowing there is no such person worthy of your trust. It is feeling that "they wouldn't like me if they knew the real me." It is becoming terrified when speaking to a group of your peers, and feeling like a fool when you get home. It is wondering why other people have so much more talent and ability than you do. It is feeling incredibly ugly and sexually unattractive. It is admitting that you have become a failure as a wife and mother. It is disliking everything about yourself and wishing, constantly wishing, you could be someone else. It is feeling unloved and unlovable and lonely and sad. It is lying in bed after the family is asleep, pondering the vast emptiness inside and longing for unconditional love. It is intense self-pity. It is reaching up in the darkness to remove a tear from the corner of your eye. *It is depression!*

There will be a few readers at this point who will have no true understanding of the experiences I am describing. They are, perhaps, the women who were "superstars" as children: they were cute babies, bright in the early school years, cheerleaders and homecoming queens and everybody's favorites in high school. For these relatively rare individuals who have never experienced the pangs of inferiority, this primary source of feminine depression will remain a bit mysterious. For the greater majority, however, personal identification with this emotional dungeon will be instantaneous. Have *you* been there? Have you drawn the same weary conclusion that you are a flop and a failure in life? If so, much of the text which follows will be addressed to your needs. *Every* item on the Sources of Depression list relates to it, one way or another.

I have said that low self-esteem is extremely common among women today; that fact was illustrated again, just moments ago. This book is being written in a quiet public library near my home (out of hearing of my telephone), and the supervising librarian approached me during a break in my work. She told me that a patron was trying to locate one of my previous books, *Hide or Seek,* and wondered if I would speak to her? A graceful woman approximately forty-five years of age was waiting for me at the counter. After introducing herself, she said, "I've been trying to find your book because I heard it deals with self-esteem. I am constantly depressed over my own inadequacy, and hoped I could find help in your writings." We talked for a half hour as she expressed the same intense longings and frustrations which I had been describing when the interruption came. If our conversation had been recorded, it would have beautifully illustrated the symptoms I hear so frequently expressed by women of all ages. Their frustration has become a *very* familiar theme song.

Now certainly I would not want to give the impression that low self-esteem is exclusively a feminine characteristic. Many men feel as insecure and worthless as do similarly troubled members of the gentle sex. In fact, low self-esteem is a threat to the entire human family, affecting children, adolescents, the elderly, all socioeconomic levels of society, and each race and ethnic culture. It can engulf anyone who feels disrespected in the eyes of other people. At least 90 percent of our self-concept is built from what we think others think about us. I can hardly respect myself, obviously, if the rest of the world seems to believe that I am dumb or ugly or lazy or boring or uncreative or undesirable.

A very old proverb reads, "No one can stand the awful knowledge that he is not needed." What wisdom is recorded in that phrase! It is not uncommon for a man to develop major illnesses within a few months following his retirement. Just knowing that his job is finished often accelerates the process of deterioration. A well known physician-author stated recently that a man who believes he has no further worth or purpose in living will be dead in eighteen months. Likewise, the most rebellious, hostile teen-agers are usually those who are bitterly disappointed with who they are and what they are becoming.

If low self-esteem is so pervasive throughout our society, then why have I emphasized its impact specifically on women? Because the "disease" of inferiority has reached epidemic proportions among females, particularly, at this time in our history. Their traditional responsibilities have become matters of disrespect and ridicule. Raising children and maintaining a home hold very little social status in most areas of the country, and women who are cast into that role often look at themselves with unconcealed disenchantment.

To understand this process, let's look at a contrived example. Suppose it suddenly became very unpopular to be a dentist. Suppose every magazine carried an article or two about the stupidity of the tooth and gums boys, making them look foolish and gauche. Suppose television commercials and dramas and comedy programs all poked fun at the same battered target. Suppose the humor associated with dentistry then died, leaving contempt and general disrespect in its place. Suppose the men in white were ignored at social gatherings and their wives were excluded from "in" group activities. Suppose dentists had difficulty hiring assistants and associates because no one wanted his friends to know he was working for a tooth fairy. What would happen if all social status were suddenly drained from the profession of dentistry? I suspect that it would soon become very difficult to get a cavity drilled and filled.

The illustration is extreme, admittedly, but the analogy to women can hardly be missed. Housewives have been teased and ridiculed and disrespected. They have been the butt of jokes and sordid humor until the subject is no longer funny. As I have spoken to family groups across the country, great frustration has been expressed by those women who have been made to feel dumb and foolish for wanting to stay at home. Those who are dedicated to their responsibilities are currently being mocked in women's magazines as "Supermoms." They have heard the prevailing opinion: "There must be something wrong with those strange creatures who seem to like domestic duties and responsibilities."

I appeared on a radio talk show in Los Angeles last week, and the militant female moderator argued that it was virtually impossible for a woman to be happy at home. The forces which have promulgated this viewpoint are everywhere at once—on television, in magazines, on radio, in newspapers, in written advertisements, in books and novels—each one hacking steadily at the confidence and satisfaction of women at home. It is not surprising, then, that American housewives are faced with the awful knowledge that they are "not needed." They would have to be deaf and blind to have missed that message.

But the decline in self-respect among women has other causes, as well. Another highly significant factor has to do with the role of beauty in our society. I documented this problem extensively in my book *Hide or Seek,* and will not take time to restate the entire issue here. It is enough to say that physical attractiveness (or the lack of it) has a profound impact on feminine self-esteem. It is very difficult to separate basic human worth from the quality of one's own body; therefore, a woman who feels ugly is almost certain to feel inferior to her peers. This pressure is greatly magnified in a highly eroticized society such as ours. Isn't it reasonable that the more steamed up a culture becomes over sex (and ours is at the boiling point), the more likely it is to reward beauty and punish ugliness? When sex becomes super-significant as it is today, then those with the least sex appeal necessarily begin to worry about their inability to compete in that marketplace. They are bankrupt in the most valuable "currency" of the day. Millions have fallen into that trap.

Advertisements have contributed immeasurably to the notion that the slightest physical flaw is cause for alarm and despair. Have you seen the magazine ad for a magic cream that promises to remove "horrid age spots"? It shows a picture of four menopausal women playing cards, and one is cringing in shame because she has an "age spot" on her naked hand. The word "horrid" is always used to describe her condition. Now seriously, folks, in view of the world's grave problems, a freckle on the paw couldn't rank very high, yet every middle-aged woman who sees that advertisement will look down at her hands with a gasp of anxiety. How can she bear the disgrace? It is horrid, no less. By cultivating this kind of nonsense, Madison Avenue has taught us to feel inferior and inadequate over the slightest physical imperfections.

A third source of low self-esteem among American women relates to basic intelligence. Simply stated, they feel dumb and stupid. Psychologists have known for decades that there is no fundamental difference in the overall level of intelligence between men and women, although there are areas of greater strength for each sex. Men tend to score higher on tests of mathematics and abstract reasoning, while women excel in language and all verbal skills. However, when the individual abilities are combined, neither sex has a clear advantage over the other. Despite this fact, women are much more inclined to doubt their own mental capacity than are men. Why? I don't know, but it is a very important factor in low self-esteem.

Incidentally, men tend to value intelligence above physical attractiveness in themselves, although both qualities are highly desired. For women, however, the opposite is true. Beauty outranks intelligence throughout life. *The reason the average woman would rather have beauty than brains is because she knows the average man can see better than he can think.* (No offense intended, gentlemen.)

In reality, low self-esteem among women may be traced to thousands of causes, most of them linked with early home life in one way or another. The adult who felt unloved or disrespected as a child will *never* fully forget the experience. As the tongue always returns to the site of a missing tooth, the human mind constantly searches and gropes for evidence of its own worthiness. Thus, childhood inferiority imposes itself on mental apparatus for decades to come.

So what are today's women doing about the problem of low self-esteem? No one can ignore it completely, any more than a severe headache can be suppressed. The pain of inferiority is incredibly intense, absolutely *demanding* the attention of its sufferer. As such, more day-by-day behavior is motivated by "ego needs" than any other factor in human experience, including the power of sex. Women who feel inferior *must* seek ways to deal with it, and the two most common coping responses today are at opposite ends of the behavioral spectrum. The feminine reader might look for her own footprints within the description of these two divergent personality patterns.

1. Withdrawal

During the fall of 1966, I accepted a position on the staff of Children's Hospital of Los Angeles, and was required to attend a general orientation session on the morning of my arrival. Everyone who has worked for a large organization is acquainted with the nature of these orientation meetings. New employees are told how to operate the telephones and about insurance and retirement programs and sick-leave benefits, etc. As you will recall, these sessions are *always* dull and boring! I think they are planned that way by the personnel departments which develop them. I can visualize an advertisement placed in the classified section of a newspaper as follows: "Wanted, Orientation Session Leader. Must have monotone voice, disinterest in life, and ability to speak while yawning. Those with sense of humor need not apply. Please contact Miss Maude Wananabee in the Personnel Department shortly after her morning nap."

As one might guess, I didn't go into the Orientation Session with any overwhelming enthusiasm or anticipation. I was directed to be in Room 203 at 9 A.M., and I arrived five minutes early. There were twelve of us to be indoctrinated that morning, and it just happened that the other eleven were women. I don't know why. Furthermore, most of the other participants looked very young—perhaps eighteen or nineteen years of age—and they were probably beginning their first secretarial or clerical jobs. Frankly, the social atmosphere was icy that day. The first hours on a new job are scary, at best, and the girls were obviously tense. Have you ever been in a small room containing twelve people where no one is talking to anybody else? It's a weird scene, reminding me of how people act in a crowded elevator. Everyone on board silently watches the numbers above the door—as though something highly informative were happening there. That was the kind of social atmosphere that prevailed at the start of our meeting: If one girl whispered a message to another standing nearby, everyone would turn to look and listen. Consequently, no one spoke unless required to do so.

There was only one hope that the twelve of us would survive the activities of the morning, and that was in the expectation that coffee would be served. I glanced around the room and spied a large coffee pot on a table in one corner. Now I don't know what caused the delay, but our indomitable leader apparently failed to get the brew started on time. She didn't even mention the coffee, but we could all hear the pot chugging and gurgling. The aroma drifted throughout the room and I knew the eleven women were thinking about it. They would turn and look at the pot when it spoke. Furthermore, there were dozens of doughnuts carefully arranged on the coffee table, and that definitely increased our interest in the northwest part of the room.

Our leader apparently didn't notice the heartfelt desire of the group. She stepped to the podium and began working her way down the forty-two-item agenda. After an interminable period of time, perhaps an hour or more, she said unenthusiastically, "Okay, people, I think we'll take a short break now, and we'll have some refreshments." But she was organized, folks. She had obviously thought this thing out in advance. She didn't just turn that mob loose to go over to the coffee pot en masse. She felt it would be a good idea for us to go one at a time. I was sitting on one end of a horseshoe table (see diagram) and she turned to the young woman in position A on the opposite side.

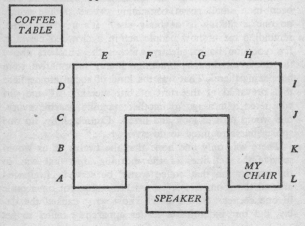

"Would you like to go get a cup of coffee?" she asked the first girl. Well, this young lady was about eighteen or nineteen years of age and was undeniably nervous about her new job. She glanced quickly around the room then dropped her eyes and said softly, "No, thank you, I don't believe I'll have any coffee." I knew very well what she was thinking. There are *many* ways you can get hurt while doing anything in front of eleven other people. She could stumble awkwardly on the way to the table. The spigot could stick on the coffee pot. She could burn herself coming back. There were just too many risks involved in the solo performance, and she "withdrew" from the challenge. I'm sure she intended to let everyone else go first and then she would change her mind and get a cup of coffee with no risk. I watched her with amusement.

The undaunted leader carried out her prearranged game plan and turned to the second girl, in position B. "Well, how about you, would you like to get some coffee?" she asked. This second girl sized up the risk and realized that she faced all the same threats as the first employee, plus one additional sanction. The "group" had spoken through that first girl and said, "We're not drinking coffee today." The pressure was too great, and she replied shyly, "No, thank you."

The girl in position C was in a tougher spot yet. We then had a unanimous vote of two to nothing against the acceptance of coffee and doughnuts. How could she defy that solidarity of opinion? She couldn't and didn't. "No, thank you!" she said discreetly.

The pressure then became enormous. Girls sitting in positions D, E, F, G, and H all declined the offer of refreshments. I couldn't believe it. There was the coffee pot, waving and beckoning to all. There were the multi-colored doughnuts, smiling and offering their services. This was to be the only oasis between two arid deserts, yet the caravan refused to drink. The offer of coffee came all the way around to where I sat, and not one person had accepted. When it became my turn, I said, "I believe I'll have a cup." I got up and walked toward the table, and *eleven women followed me over there!*

I looked over my shoulder and here came the entire group. To be a gentleman I stepped back and let the ladies go first, and it took me fifteen minutes to get to the coffee pot!

Isn't it amazing how terrified we are of each other? We cower in fear that we will bring ridicule down upon us, even when the act in question is of no moral or social significance. As in this example, we usually take the safest and quietest route, even when the issue is as silly as "To doughnut or not to doughnut!" The genuine withdrawer will cower backward in fear and trembling. He will never say a word in a group unless the subject is innocuous and the thought has been carefully screened. He will run no social risks that aren't absolutely necessary. He will spend much of his time alone and will avoid any activity that might prove threatening. He will peek out at the world going by, but will rarely let his hidden self be observed, either publicly or in private. He will be excessively meek. (Jackie Vernon said, "The meek will inherit the earth because they'll be too timid to refuse it." I think he's right.)

And, of course, the painful part of withdrawing is the self-pity which almost always accompanies it. Intense personal sorrow is a constant companion of this life style, bringing with it those destructive little comments spoken in the inner chambers of the mind: "I knew you'd blow it," and "You never do anything right," and "Wouldn't you know it would happen to me," and "Why!? Why!? Why?!" Even the friends of a self-pitier are selected for their willingness to commiserate in the tragedies of daily living.

Self-pity is both addictive and highly contagious. It spreads like wildfire within a family, neighborhood, or church congregation. It is also exhausting, leaving its victims unmotivated, tired, bored, and miserable. And more and more commonly, this form of despair among women leads to the ultimate in personal hatred, suicide itself.

In all, withdrawing is not a very successful approach to inferiority. It is the most stressful and the least effective of all the ego defenses. In reality, it is *no* defense. For centuries, however, withdrawal has been the most common personality pattern among women.

2. Fighting

I was recently invited to appear on a live television program in Los Angeles to discuss the subject of self-esteem in women. No mention was made of any other professional being asked to appear with me, so I assumed it was to be a solo shot. When I arrived at the studio, however, I was taken to the Green Room and introduced to a woman who was identified as the "other guest." After mumbling "hello," she slumped in a chair and neither looked at me nor spoke again unless I asked her a direct question. It was clear from the scowl on her face that this was not Polly Personality to be sharing the camera with me. Then I noticed a large bronze medallion hanging around her neck, with a clenched fist thrust upward into the traditional symbol for female. It began to be obvious that my opinions might tend to differ a bit with those of the "other guest." (I'm amazingly perceptive at reading the subtle clues around me.)

"What kind of work do you do?" I asked with genuine interest.

"I run consciousness-raising groups for women," she replied.

The creaking of her jaw into the closed position told me she intended to offer no further details. That's about as far as our conversation got before we were ushered to the set. During the thirty-minute broadcast which followed, her venom and hatred for men poured forth. She reiterated all of the familiar concepts of the most militant feminists and attacked everything remotely traditional about the home, child rearing, and marriage. I presented the opposing viewpoint with equal candor, of course, and stated that anger and hostility were not the best solutions for feelings of inferiority and inadequacy. "No!" she said with great emotion. "We *need* the anger!" (See the postscript to this story on page 142.)

It was clearly the objective of my toothy friend to spread hostility among women far and wide. She exuded anger out her fingertips and reminded me of an ill-tempered bulldog. Her motive for propagating the hatred of men was partially financial, since her consciousness-raising groups obviously spent much of their time in man-hating activities. But what source of energy powers the anger of the women's movement at large? Why has hostility become so characteristic of many "liberation" groups today? The answer is found primarily in feelings of inferiority. Anger is another increasingly prevalent way of handling all forms of frustration.

While withdrawal has gone out of style among those who feel inferior, anger is in its heyday. Everyone who has an axe to grind is supposed to lash out at his oppressors with a clenched fist. Whether it be the black civil rights advocate, or the Brown Berets, or the Jewish Defense League, or the Gay Liberation Movement, or the parents against bussing, or the Veterans Against the War, or the eighth grade class at Woodrow Wilson Junior High School, everyone is mad at somebody. And when it's all put together, we have a society in the throes of violence. The anger of the Women's Liberation Movement is part of this pattern.

Withdrawing and fighting are only two of the familiar responses to inferiority but these are the most common. It is an unfortunate pattern, too, because they are both extreme approaches to the problem. One lies at one end of the pendulum and the other far out to the other side. Both are overreactions. Neither is very healthy. There is a better response to low self-esteem, as we will see in the following sections.

Summary

Joyce Landorf, the gifted authoress of *His Stubborn Love,* recently asked people to answer the following question: What would you change about women in general if you could wave some sort of magic wand? My answer, which is now published with the other replies in her book *The Fragrance of Beauty,* is quoted below:

> If I could write a prescription for the women of the world, I would provide each one of them with a healthy dose of self-esteem and personal worth (taken three times a day until the symptoms disappear). I have no doubt that this is their greatest need . . . . If women felt genuinely respected in their role as wives and mothers, they would not need to abandon it for something better. If they felt *equal* with men in personal worth, they would not need to be equivalent to men in responsibility. If they could only bask in the dignity and status granted them by the Creator, then their femininity would be valued as their greatest asset, rather than scorned as an old garment to be discarded. Without question, the future of a nation depends on how it sees its women, and I hope we will teach our little girls to be glad they were chosen by God for the special pleasures of womanhood.[1]

This understanding of the feminine world was certainly verified by my questionnaire on the Sources of Depression in women. The wives and mothers who participated in this inquiry did not appear to be suffering from low self-esteem. They were outwardly social and pleasant, laughing and interacting with one another.

Yet when given an opportunity to reflect their true feelings in confidence, self-doubt rose to the surface. One of those young women later came to me for counseling and wept for more than an hour as she tried to express the inexpressible anguish of inferiority. Near the end of our session I asked her if she had ever shared these feelings with her husband. Her reply was typical, "I have been married for eight years, but my husband has no idea that I feel so inadequate!"

Inferiority is the best kept secret of the year, yet it is one which wives most wish their husbands comprehended. Perhaps the pages which follow will help convey that message.

Questions and Answers

Each of the items in the Sources of Depression Questionnaire has been the subject for many of my addresses and lectures in recent years. Following those presentations have been spontaneous question and answer sessions between the audience and me. Some of the specific issues raised and my replies are reproduced below. (I'm much more effective with True or False and multiple choice questions than those presented here, but I'm rarely let off the hook that easily.)

Question: How do feelings of inferiority get started? It seems as though I've always felt inadequate, but I can't remember where it all began.

Answer: You don't remember it because your self-doubt originated during your earliest days of conscious existence. A little child is born with an irrepressible inclination to question his own worth; it is as "natural" as his urge to walk and talk. At first, it is a primitive assessment of his place in the home, and then it extends outward to his early social contacts beyond the front door. These initial impressions of who he is have a profound effect on his developing personality, particularly if the experiences are painful. It is not uncommon for a pre-kindergartener to have concluded already that he is terribly ugly, incredibly dumb, unloved, unneeded, foolish, or strange.

These early feelings of inadequacy may remain relatively tranquil and subdued during the elementary school years. They lurk just below the conscious mind and are never far from awareness. But the child with the greatest self-doubts constantly "accumulates" evidence of his inferiority during these middle years. Each failure is recorded in vivid detail. Every unkind remark is inscribed in his memory. Rejection and ridicule scratch and nick his delicate ego all through the "quiet" years. Then it happens! He enters adolescence and his world explodes from within. All of the accumulated evidence is resurrected and propelled into his conscious mind with volcanic forcefulness. He will deal with that devastating experience for the rest of his life. Have you done the same? (Incidentally, I have recorded a set of six cassette tapes in an album entitled *Preparing for Adolescence*, which is designed to help pre-teens and early adolescents adjust to the feelings I have described. See the list on p. 189.)

Question: I have a friend who was married for nine years before her husband left her for another woman. I think she was a loving and devoted wife, yet she seemed to feel that the break-up of her marriage was her own fault. As a result, her self-esteem disintegrated and has never recovered. Is this a typical reaction?

Answer: It has always been surprising for me to observe how often the wounded marriage partner—the person who was clearly the victim of the other's irresponsibility—is the one who suffers the greatest pangs of guilt and inferiority. How strange that the one who tried to hold things together in the face of obvious rejection often finds herself wondering, "How did I fail him? . . . I just wasn't woman enough to hold my man . . . I am 'nothing' or he wouldn't have left . . . If only I had been more exciting as a sexual partner . . . I drove him to it . . . I wasn't pretty enough . . . I didn't deserve him in the first place."

The blame for marital disintegration is seldom the fault of the husband or the wife alone. It takes two to tango, as they say, and there is always some measure of shared blame for a divorce. However, when one marriage partner makes up his mind to behave irresponsibly, to become involved extramaritally, or to run from his family commitments and obligations, he usually seeks to justify his behavior by magnifying the failures of his spouse. "You didn't meet my needs, so I had to satisfy them somewhere else," is a familiar accusation. By increasing the guilt of his partner in this way, he reduces his own culpability. For a husband or wife with low self-esteem, these charges and recriminations are accepted as fact when hurled his way. "Yes, it was my fault. I drove you to it!" Thus, the victim assumes the full responsibility for his partner's irresponsibility, and self-worth shatters.

I would not recommend that your friend sit around hating the memory of her husband. Bitterness and resentment are emotional cancers that rot us from within. However, if I were counseling her I would encourage her to examine the facts carefully. Answers to these questions should be sought: "Despite my human frailties, did I value my marriage and try to preserve it? Did my husband decide to destroy it and then seek justification for his actions? Was I given a fair chance to resolve the areas of greatest irritation? Could I have held him even if I had made all the changes he wanted? Is it reasonable that I should hate myself for this thing that has happened?"

Your friend should know that social rejection breeds inferiority and self-pity in enormous proportions. And rejection by the one you love, particularly, is *the* most powerful destroyer of self-esteem in the entire realm of human experience. She might be helped to see herself as a victim of this process, rather than a worthless failure at the game of love.

Question: You mentioned the relationship between self-esteem and one's physical body. I have never felt beautiful or even attractive to the opposite sex. Does this explain why I am *extremely* modest, even being ashamed to be seen in a bathing suit?

Answer: Modesty has three basic origins. First, it is built into our fallen human nature. After sinning in the Garden of Eden, Adam and Eve's eyes "were opened and they knew that they were naked; and they sewed fig leaves together, and made themselves aprons." To a varying degree within the descendants of Adam, we have inherited this same sensitivity about our bodies. The current trend toward public nudity goes cross-grained to this nature and requires some "getting used to" by those who first try it. I overheard a vacuous girl sitting near me in a cafeteria recently, as she described her sexual experience to her companions. She spoke in loud, unguarded tones about her attempted "changeover" from a heterosexual to a homosexual status. "I still feel a bit strange walking around nude in front of my friends," she said, "but I'm trying to get used to it." Her conscience and her God-given modesty were obviously being violated by the "mod" attitudes she was trying to adopt. I fear she will pay a heavy price for the avant garde ideas she has been sold.

Second, modesty is a product of early home life. Those who were taught to conceal themselves compulsively in front of other family members usually carry that excessive modesty even into their marital relationships. It can turn legitimate sexual experiences into a self-conscious obligation.

The third source of extreme modesty is the one you mentioned, and it is probably the most powerful. Those who are ashamed of their bodies are highly motivated to conceal them. One of the greatest fears among junior high students is that they will have to disrobe and shower in front of their peers. Boys and girls alike are terrified by the possibility of ridicule for their lack of development (or precociousness). This embarrassment is often retained in the adult years with feelings of inferiority stamped all over it. For example, a very common reaction among women who feel unattractive is the insistence on having sexual relations in the dark. They are often extremely inflexible on this matter, even though their husbands are visually oriented and prefer to look while they love. This simple difference in viewpoints has undoubtedly been argued in a million bedrooms.

Incidentally, medical examinations are extremely distasteful for those who bear this kind of modesty. Even for those who are less sensitive about their bodies, a routine "physical" can be murder. Who hasn't felt a bit strange carrying a urine specimen through a crowded waiting room, or felt like Lady Godiva sitting side saddle on an examining table?

Question: I know a woman who needs people so badly, but she unintentionally drives them away. She talks too much and constantly complains and makes everyone want to run from her. I know she has a terrible inferiority complex, but I could help her if she would let me. How can I tell her about these irritating faults without making her feel even worse about herself?

Answer: You do it the way porcupines make love: *very*, very carefully. Let me offer a general principle that has thousands of applications in dealing with people, including the situation you have posed. *The right to criticize must be earned, even if the advice is constructive in nature.* Before you are entitled to tinker with another person's self-esteem, you are obligated *first* to demonstrate your own respect for him as a person. This is accomplished through an atmosphere of love and kindness and human warmth. Then when a relationship of confidence has been carefully constructed, you will have earned the right to discuss a potentially threatening topic. Your motives have thereby been clarified.

This principle is in direct opposition to the current mania for "honesty." One woman walks into the home of another and says, "It is smelly in here. You should air it out once in a while." Or a husband tells his wife, "I don't want to be mean, dear, but you're really getting wrinkly around the eyes." Honesty? Sure, but what a price to pay for it. *Honesty which does not have the best interest of the hearer at heart is a cruel form of selfishness.*

In response to your specific question, I would suggest that you invest some effort in building a healthy relationship with your verbose friend, and then feed her your suggestions in very small doses. And remember all the while that someone, somewhere, would like to straighten out a few of your flaws, too. We all have them.

Question: What is the most common drug prescribed in America today?

Answer: It is Valium, which is a muscle-relaxant having the effect of a tranquilizer. The need for these prescriptions tells us something about the universal tensions and pressures in our society . . . and the inability of our citizens to cope with them.

Question: My wife has been severely depressed for nearly three months. What kind of treatment or therapy would you recommend for her?

Answer: Get her to a physician, probably an internist, as soon as possible. This kind of prolonged depression can have serious medical and psychological consequences, yet it is usually very responsive to treatment. Antidepressant drugs are highly effective in controlling most cases of severe depression. Of course, the medication will not correct the circumstances which precipitated her original problem, and that brings us back to the subject for our present discussion.

CHAPTER FOUR

Fatigue
and Time Pressure

Flip Wilson once said, "If I had my entire life to live over, I doubt if I'd have the strength." There must be many women who agree with him, for *Fatigue and Time Pressure* ranked as the second most frequent cause for depression among those completing my questionnaire. As I have journeyed across the United States, from the metropolitan centers to the farms of Iowa, I have found extremely busy people running faster and faster down the road to exhaustion. We have become a nation of huffers and puffers, racing through the day and moonlighting into the night. Even our recreation is marked by this breakneck pace.

How frequently does your head whirl and spin with the obligations of an impossible "to do" list? "I simply must get the bills paid this morning and the grocery shopping can't wait another day. And my children! I've had so little time to be with them lately that we hardly seem like a family anymore. Maybe I can read them a story tonight. And I mustn't neglect my own body; exercise is important and I've got to find time for that. Perhaps I could 'Jump Along with Jack' on television each morning. My annual physical is overdue, too. And I ought to be reading more. Everyone knows that it's important to keep your mind active, so I just shouldn't neglect the printed page. If I could get into bed an hour earlier each night I could do plenty of reading. And we really should be taking more time to maintain our spiritual lives. That's one area we cannot afford to neglect. And what about our social obligations? We can't expect to have friends if we never get together. The Johnsons have had us over twice, now, and I know they're waiting for us to reciprocate. We'll just have to set a date and keep it, that's all. And there are so many things that need fixing and repairing on the house. And the income tax is due next month . . . I'd better block out some time for that. And I . . . excuse me, the phone is ringing."

So we're too busy; everyone can see that. But what does a hectic pace have to do with depression? Just this: every obligation which we shirk is a source of guilt. When there are more commitments than we can possibly handle, then self-esteem is further damaged by each failure. "I'm really a lousy parent; I'm too exhausted to be a good wife; I'm disorganized and confused; I'm out of touch with the world around me and I don't have any real friends; even God is displeased with me." Truly, overextended lives contribute to emotional pathology in numerous ways. It was this source of frustration that the women reflected on my questionnaire.

Vince Lombardi, the late, great football coach for the Green Bay Packers, once gave an inspired speech to his team at the beginning of the fall season. His comments were recorded that day, and have considerable applicability to our theme at this point. Coach Lombardi was discussing the impact of exhaustion on human courage, and he made this brief statement: "Fatigue makes cowards of us all!" How right he was. Physical depletion renders us less able to cope with the noisiness of children, the dishwasher that won't work, and the thousands of other minor irritations of everyday living. It is also said, *when you are tired you are attacked by ideas you thought you had conquered long ago.* Perhaps this explains why women (and men) who are grossly overworked become cowards—whining, griping, and biting those whom they love the most.

If fatigue and time pressure produce such a strain, then why do we permit ourselves to become so busy? Well, for one thing, everyone apparently thinks his hectic pace is a temporary problem. I have heard all the reasons why "things are kind of tough right now." Here are the four most common for the young family:

1. Jerry just started this new business, you know, so it'll take a few years to get it going.
2. Well, Pete is in school for two more years, so I've been trying to work to help out with the finances.
3. We have a new baby in our house and you know what that means.
4. We just bought a new house, which we're fixing up ourselves.

To hear them tell it, there is a slower day coming, as soon as the present obligations are met. But you know it is an illusion. Their "temporary" pressures are usually sandwiched back to back with other temporary pressures, gradually developing into a long-term style of living. My secretary taped a little note to her typewriter which read, "As soon as the rush is over, I'm going to have a nervous breakdown. I've earned it, I deserve it, and nobody is going to keep me from having it." Time proves, however, that the rush is never over. As the Beatles said of women in their song "Lady Madonna," "See how they run!"

No one "runs" much faster than the mother of multiple

preschool children. Not only is she rushed from morning to night, but she experiences an unusual kind of emotional stress as well. Youngsters between two and five years of age have an uncanny ability to unravel an adult nervous system. Maybe it is listening to the constant diarrhea of words that wears Mom down to utter exhaustion. Hasn't every mother in the world had the following "conversation" with her child at least a million times?

Johnny: Can I have a cookie, Mom? Huh, Mom? Can I? Can I have one, Mom? Why can't I have one? Huh? Huh, Mom? Can I? Mom? Mom, can I? Can I have a cookie now?

Mom: No, Johnny, it's too close to lunch time.

Johnny: Just one, Mom? Can't I have just one little cookie now? Huh? Can I? I will eat my lunch. Okay, Mom? Okay? I will eat all my lunch. OK? Can I? Just one? Spotty would like one, too. Dogs like cookies, too, don't they, Mom? Don't they? Don't dogs like cookies, too?

Mom: Yes, Johnny. I guess dogs like cookies, too.

Johnny: Can Spotty and I have one? Huh? Can we?

Although "mom" began her day with a guarded optimism about life, these questions have reduced her to a lump of putty by 4 P.M.

My wife and I observed this process in action while sitting in a restaurant in Hawaii last summer. A young couple and their four-year-old son were seated near us, and the child was rattling like a machine gun. If he stopped even to breathe, I couldn't detect it. Nonsensical questions and comments were bubbling forth from his inexhaustible fountain of verbiage. It was easy to see the harassment on his parents' faces, for they were about to explode from the constant onslaught of noise. Finally, the mother leaned over to her son and without moving her lips she sent this unmistakable message through her clenched teeth . . . one syllable at a time: "Shut! Up! Shut! Up! Don't—say—one—more—word! If—you—say—one—more—word—I—will—scream!" We had to smile, for her frustration was vaguely familiar to us. This young woman told us at the checkstand that her verbose son had talked from morning to night for two years, and her composure teetered on the brink of disintegration. As we left the restaurant and walked in opposite directions, we could hear the child's fading words: "Who was that, Mom? Who were those people? Were they nice people, Mom? Do you know those nice people, Mom. . . ?"

Mothers of children under three years of age are particularly in need of loving support from their husbands. It has certainly been true in our home. How well I remember the day my wife put Ryan, then four months old, on the dressing table to change his diapers. As soon as she removed the wet garments, he made like a fountain and initiated the wall and a picture of Little Boy Blue. Shirley had no sooner repaired the damage than the telephone rang; while she was gone, Ryan was struck by a sudden attack of projectile diarrhea, and he machine-gunned his crib and the rest of the nursery. By the time my patient wife had bathed her son and scoured the room, she was near exhaustion. She dressed Ryan in clean, sweet-smelling clothes and put him over her shoulder affectionately. At that moment he deposited his breakfast down her neck and into her undergarments. She told me that evening that she was going to re-read her motherhood contract to see if days like that were written in the fine print. Needless to say, the family went out to dinner that night.

No discussion of maternal fatigue would be complete without mentioning the early evening hours—unquestionably the toughest part of the day for the mother of small children. Much has been written lately about the international "energy crisis," but there is nothing on the globe to parallel the shortage of energy in a young mother between 6:00 and 9:00 P.M.! The dinner is over and the dishes are stacked. She is already tired, but now she has to get the troops in bed. She gives them their baths and pins on the diapers and brushes their teeth and puts on the pajamas and reads a story and says the prayers and brings them seven glasses of water. These tasks would not be so difficult if the children *wanted* to go to bed. They most certainly do not, however, and develop extremely clever techniques for resistance and postponement. It is a pretty dumb kid who can't extend this ten-minute process into an hour-long tug of war. And when it's all finished and mom staggers through the nursery door and leans against the wall, she is then supposed to shift gears and greet her romantic lover in her own bedroom. Fat chance!

Let's look at the problem of fatigue and time pressure exclusively from the perspective of children. How do they cope with the constant rush and scurry within the family? First, children are often aware of the tension, even when we adults have learned to ignore or deny it. A father recently told me he was putting on his toddler's shoes, and he didn't even realize that he was rushing to complete the job quickly. His three-year-old quietly looked up at him and said, "Are we in a hurry again, Daddy?" Zap! The arrow struck in his heart. "Yes, son, I guess we're always in a hurry," he said with a sigh of regret.

The viewpoint of children was beautifully represented by a little nine-year-old girl, who composed her idea of what a grandmother is supposed to be. This piece was submitted by a nurse, Juanita Nelson, and appeared in the employee newspaper at Children's Hospital of Los Angeles. I think you will appreciate the incredible insight of this third grade girl.

What's A Grandmother?
by a third grader

A grandmother is a lady who has no children of her own. She likes other people's little girls and boys. A grandfather is a man grandmother. He goes for walks with the boys, and they talk about fishing and stuff like that.

Grandmothers don't have to do anything except to be there. They're old so they shouldn't play hard or run. It is enough if they drive us to the market where the pretend horse is, and have a lot of dimes ready. Or if they take us for walks, they should slow down past things like pretty leaves and caterpillars. They should never say "hurry-up."

Usually grandmothers are fat, but not too fat to tie your shoes. They wear glasses and funny underwear. They can take their teeth and gums off.

Grandmothers don't have to be smart, only answer questions like, "Why isn't God married?" and "How come dogs chase cats!"

Grandmothers don't talk baby talk like visitors do, because it is hard to understand. When they read to us they don't skip or mind if it is the same story over again.

Everybody should try to have a grandmother, especially if you don't have television, because they are the only grown-ups who have time.

How's that for sheer wisdom from the pen of a child? This little girl has shown us the important role played by grandparents in the lives of small children . . . especially grandparents who can take their teeth and gums off! (I am reminded of the time my eleven-month-old daughter was given a hard cookie by a little boy. His older sister scolded, "She can't eat that, you dummy! She has rubber teeth!") Regardless of the condition of their molars, grandmothers and grandfathers can be invaluable to the world of little people. For one thing, "They are the only grown-ups who have time."

It is interesting that our little authoress made two references to time pressure. How badly children need adults who can go for casual walks and talk about fishing and stuff like that . . . and slow down to look at pretty leaves and caterpillars . . . and answer questions about God and the nature of the world as it is. I dealt with this responsibility in my book *Hide or Seek,* and feel my message should be repeated here.

Why do dedicated parents have to be reminded to be sensitive to the needs of their children, anyway? Shouldn't this be the natural expression of their love and concern? Yes, it should, but Mom and Dad have some problems of their own. They are pushed to the limits of their endurance by the pressure of time. Dad is holding down three jobs and he huffs and puffs to keep up with it all. Mom never has a free minute, either. Tomorrow night, for example, she is having eight guests for dinner and she only has this one evening to clean the house, go to the market, arrange the flowers for the centerpiece, and put the hem in the dress she will wear. Her "to do" list is three pages long and she already has a splitting headache from it all. She opens a can of "Spaghetti-Os" for the kids' supper and hopes the troops will stay out of her hair. About 7 P.M., little Larry tracks down his perspiring mother and says, "Look what I just drawed, Mom." She glances downward and says, "Uh huh," obviously thinking about something else.

Ten minutes later, Larry asks her to get him some juice. She complies but resents his intrusion. She is behind schedule and her tension is mounting. Five minutes later he interrupts again, this time wanting her to reach a toy that sits on the top shelf of the closet. She stands looking down at him for a moment and then hurries down the hall to meet his demand, mumbling as she goes. But as she passes his bedroom door, she notices that he has spread his toys all over the floor and made a mess with the glue. Mom explodes. She screams and threatens and shakes Larry till his teeth rattle.

Does this drama sound familiar? It should, for "routine panic" is becoming an American way of life. . . There was a time when a man didn't fret if he missed a stage coach; he'd just catch it next month. Now if a fellow misses a section of a revolving door he's thrown into despair! But guess who is the inevitable loser from this breathless life-style? It's the little guy who is leaning against the wall with his hands in the pockets of his blue jeans. He misses his father during the long day and tags around after him at night, saying, "Play ball, Dad!" But Dad is pooped. Besides, he has a briefcase full of work to be done. Mom had promised to take him to the park this afternoon but then she had to go to that Women's Auxiliary meeting at the last minute. The lad gets the message—his folks are busy again. So he drifts into the family room and watches two hours of pointless cartoons and reruns on television.

Children just don't fit into a "to do" list very well. It takes time to introduce them to good books—it takes time to listen, once more, to the skinned-knee episode and talk about the bird with the broken wing. These are the building blocks of esteem, held together with the mortar of love. But they seldom materialize amidst busy timetables. Instead, crowded lives produce fatigue—and fatigue produces irritability—and irritability produces indifference—and indifference can be interpreted by the child as a lack of genuine affection and personal esteem.

As the commercial says, "Slow down, America!" What is your rush, anyway? Don't you know your

children will be gone so quickly and you will have
nothing but blurred memories of those years when
they needed you? I'm not suggesting that we invest
our entire adult lives into the next generation, nor
must everyone become parents. But once those children are here, they had better fit into our schedule
somewhere. This is, however, a lonely message at
the present time in our society. Others are telling
Mom to go to work—have a career—do her own
thing—turn her babies over to employees of the state
working in child-care centers. Let someone else discipline, teach, and guide her toddler. While she's at
it, though, she'd better hope that her "someone else"
gets across the message of esteem and worth to that
pudgy little butterball who waves "good-bye" to his
mommy each morning.[1]

Summary and Recommendations

From this discussion of the universal problem . . .
fatigue and time pressure . . . what related concepts do
wives most wish their husbands understood? It is my
belief that feminine depression associated with the hustle
and bustle of living could be reduced significantly if
men comprehended and accepted the three ideas which
follow:

1. For some strange reason, human beings (and particularly women), tolerate stresses and pressure much
more easily if at least one other person knows they are
enduring it. This principle is filed under the category of
"human understanding," and it is highly relevant to
housewives. The frustrations of raising small children and
handling domestic duties would be much more manage-
able if their husbands acted like they comprehended it
all. Even if a man does nothing to change the situation,
simply his awareness that his wife did an admirable

job today will make it easier for her to repeat the assignment tomorrow. Instead, the opposite usually occurs. At least eight million husbands will stumble into the same unforgiveable question tonight: "What did you do all day, Dear?" The very nature of the question implies that the little woman has been sitting on her rear-end watching television and drinking coffee since arising at noon! The little woman could kill him for saying it.

Everyone needs to know that he is respected for the way he meets his responsibilities. Husbands get this emotional nurture through job promotions, raises in pay, annual evaluations, and incidental praise during the work day. Women at home get it from their husbands—if they get it at all. The most unhappy wives and mothers are often those who handle their fatigue and time pressure in solitude, and their men are never very sure why they always act so tired.

2. Most women will agree that the daily tasks of running a household can be managed; it is the accumulating projects that break their backs. Periodically, someone has to clean the stove and refrigerator, and replace the shelf paper, and wax the floors and clean the windows. These kinds of cyclical responsibilities are always waiting in line for the attention of a busy mother, and prevent her from ever feeling "caught up." It is my belief that *most* families can afford to hire outside help to handle these projects, and the money would be well spent for such a purpose.

The suggestion of hiring domestic help may seem highly impractical in this inflationary economy where everyone has too much "month" left at the end of the money. However, I am merely recommending that each family reevaluate how it spends its resources. This matter was first discussed in *Hide or Seek,* and at the risk of redundance, I am again quoting from that remarkable volume:

Most Americans maintain a "priority list" of things to purchase when enough money has been saved for that purpose. They plan ahead to reupholster the sofa or carpet the dining-room floor or buy a newer car. However, it is my conviction that domestic help for the mother of small children should appear on that priority list too. Without it, she is sentenced to the same responsibility day in and day out, seven days a week. For several years, she is unable to escape the unending burden of dirty diapers, runny noses, and unwashed dishes. It is my belief that she will do a more efficient job in those tasks and be a better mother if she can share the load with someone else occasionally. More explicitly, I feel she should get out of the house completely for one day a week, doing something for sheer enjoyment. This seems more important to the happiness of the home than buying new drapes or a power saw for Dad.

But how can middle-class families afford house-cleaning and baby-sitting services in these inflationary days? It can best be accomplished by using competent high-school students instead of older adults. I would suggest that a call be placed to the counseling office of the nearest senior high school. Tell the counselor that you need a mature, third-year student to do some cleaning. Do not reveal that you're looking for a regular employee. When the referred girl arrives, try her out for a day and see how she handles responsibility. If she's very efficient, offer her a weekly job. If she is slow and flighty, thank her for coming and call for another student that following week. There is a remarkable difference in maturity level between high-school girls, and you'll eventually find one who works like an adult.

Incidentally, if your husband is saving for that new power saw, it might be better to eliminate one of your own priority items the first time around. Either way, don't tell him I sent you![2]

3. Husbands *and* wives should constantly guard against the scourge of overcommitment. Even worthwhile and enjoyable activities become damaging when they consume the last ounce of energy or the remaining free moments in the day. Though it is rarely possible for a busy family, everyone needs to waste some time every now and then—to walk along kicking rocks and thinking pleasant thoughts. Men need time to putter in the garage and women need to pluck their eyebrows and do the girlish things again. But as I have described, the whole world seems to conspire against such reconstructive activities. Even our vacations are hectic: "We have to reach St. Louis by sundown or we'll lose our reservations."

I can provide a simple prescription for a happier, healthier life, but it must be implemented by the individual family. *You* must resolve to slow your pace; you must learn to say "no" gracefully; you must resist the temptation to chase after more pleasures, more hobbies, more social entanglements; you must "hold the line" with the tenacity of a tackle for a professional football team, blocking out the intruders and defending the home team. In essence, three questions should be asked about every new activity which presents itself: Is it worthy of our time? What will be eliminated if it is added? What will be its impact on our family life? My suspicion is that most of the items in our busy day would score rather poorly on this three-item test.

You'll have to excuse me now; I'm late for an appointment. . . .

Questions and Answers

Question: How do you feel about employment for mothers of preschool children? What part does their "outside" work play in the problem of fatigue and time pressure?

Answer: It is reasonable, isn't it, that one cannot carve forty choice hours from the week for an investment in a job without imposing "fatigue and time pressure" on the remaining portion. Thus, I am strongly opposed to the mothers of *preschool* children holding down full-time employment in situations which do not require it. Yet we are currently witnessing a vast movement of women into the commercial world with numerous consequences for the home and family. As stated before, every disenchanted housewife is being offered the same solution to her low self-esteem: get a job, have a career, and do your own thing. Almost half of the women in this country are currently employed (30,370,000, according to government figures published in 1973) and the totals are rising. My viewpoint on this national trend is not likely to win many admirers within certain circles, but I can't remain silent on so important a topic. *In short, I believe that this abandonment of the home is our gravest and most dangerous mistake as a nation!*

Certainly, there are stressful financial situations which demand that a wife go to work to help support the family. And there are more serious marital disruptions where the husband either cannot work or is removed from the home for one reason or another. These problems obviously require the financial contribution of the women involved. However, to sell the concept across America that every female who isn't "working" is being cheated and exploited is a lie with enormous consequences.

This falsehood is vigorously supported by two other myths which are equally foolish. The first is that *most* mothers of small children can work all day and still come home and meet their family obligations—perhaps even better than they could if they remained at home. Nonsense! There is only so much energy within the human body for expenditure during each twenty-four hours, and when it is invested in one place it is not available for use in another. It is highly improbable that the *average* woman can arise early in the morning and get her family fed and located for the day, then work from 9:00 to 5:00, drive home from 5:01 to 5:30, and still have the energy to assault her "home-work" from 5:31 until midnight. Oh, she may cook dinner and handle the major household chores, but few women alive are equipped with the superstrength necessary at the end of a workday to meet the emotional needs of their children, to train and guide and discipline, to build self-esteem, to teach the true values of life, and beyond all that, to maintain a healthy marital relationship as well. Perhaps the task can be accomplished for a week or a month, or even a season. But for years on end? I simply don't believe it. To the contrary, I have observed that exhausted wives and mothers become irritable, grouchy, and frustrated, setting the stage for conflict within the home.

Incidentally, *busy* wives must summon every ounce of creativity if they are to meet their many commitments. I know one mother who has developed a unique "stalling" device for use when she is late with the preparation of dinner. She rushes into the kitchen a few minutes before her husband arrives home from work, and places one sliced onion in the heated oven. When he walks through the front door, he is greeted by a pleasant aroma of, perhaps, beef stew or enchilada pie. He is so pleased by the obvious progress in the kitchen that he settles down to read his paper and await the final product. Of course, she occasionally has to explain why tuna fish sandwiches made the house smell like onion-something-or-other.

The second myth standing on wobbly legs is that small children (those under five years of age) don't really need the extensive nurturing and involvement of their mothers, anyway. If this falsehood were accurate, it would conveniently expunge all guilt from the consciences of working women. But it simply won't square with scientific knowledge. I attended a national conference on child development held recently in Miami, Florida. Virtually every report of research presented during that three-day meeting ended with the same conclusion: the mother-child relationship is absolutely vital to healthy development of children. The final speaker of the conference, a well-known authority in this field, explained that the Russian government is currently abandoning its child-care network because they have observed the same inescapable fact: employees of the State simply cannot replace the one-to-one influence of a mother with her own child. The speaker concluded his remarks by saying that feminine responsibilities are so vital to the next generation that the future of our nation actually depends on how we "see" our women. I agree.

But my intense personal opinions on this matter of "preschool mothering" are not only based on scientific evidence and professional experience. My views have also been grealty influenced within my own home. Our two children are infinitely complex, as are all children, and my wife and I want to guide the formative years ourselves. Danae is nine years old. She will be an adolescent in four more seasons, and I am admittedly jealous of anything robbing me of these remaining days of her childhood. Every moment is precious to me. Ryan is now four (having had a birthday since the book began). Not only is he in constant motion, but he is also in a state of rapid physical and emotional change. At times it is almost frightening to see how dynamic is the development of my little toddler. When I leave home for a four- or five-day speaking trip, Ryan is a noticeably different child upon my return. The building blocks for his future emotional and physical stability are clearly being laid moment by moment, stone upon stone, precept upon precept. Now I ask you who disagree with what I have written; to whom am I going to submit the task of guiding that unfolding process of development? Who will care enough to make the necessary investment if my wife and

I are too busy for the job? What babysitter will take our place? What group-oriented facility can possibly provide the *individual* love and guidance which Ryan needs and deserves? Who will represent my values and beliefs to my son and daughter and be ready to answer their questions during the peak of interest? To whom will I surrender the prime-time experiences of their day? The rest of the world can make its own choice, but as for me and my house, we welcome the opportunity to shape the two little lives which have been loaned to us. And I worry about a nation which calls that task "unrewarding and unfulfilling and boring."

I know that kids can frustrate and irritate their parents, as I have described, but the rewards of raising them far outweigh the cost. Besides, nothing worth having ever comes cheap, anyway.

Question: Are you saying, then, that every woman should become a wife and mother, regardless of her other desires?

Answer: Certainly not. A woman should feel free to choose the direction her life will take. In no sense should she be urged to raise a family and abandon her own career or educational objectives, if this is not her desire. Furthermore, I regret the "old maid" image which frightens young women into marrying the first fleeting opportunity which presents itself. My strong criticism, then, is not with those who choose nonfamily life styles for themselves. Rather, it is aimed at those who abandon their parental responsibility *after* the choice has been made.

CHAPTER FIVE

Loneliness, Isolation, and Boredom and Absence of Romantic Love in Marriage

It is altogether fitting that the women completing my questionnaire would rank their third and fourth most common sources of depression in a dead-even tie. These items are inseparably linked in many other ways as well. I am referring to the familiar despair associated with *Loneliness, Isolation, and Boredom,* along with its related malady, *Absence of Romantic Love in My Marriage.* I doubt if there is a marriage counselor alive who has gone through a single day of his practice without hearing about these twin complaints.

A closer look at the women's responses reveals a highly significant trend among American housewives. Fully one-third of the group ranked three items within the top five (*Low Self-Esteem, Loneliness, Isolation, and Boredom,* and *Absence of Romantic Love in My Marriage*). The ladies were saying in effect: (1) I don't like myself; (2) I have no meaningful relationships outside my home; (3) I am not even close to the man I love. These three categories obviously encompass the whole world! These young, attractive wives and mothers admitted to being emotionally isolated from all other human beings on earth! And therein lies the greatest source of feminine discontent in twentieth-century America.

Feelings of self-worth and acceptance, which provide the cornerstone of a healthy personality, can be obtained from only *one* source. It cannot be bought or manufactured. Self-esteem is only generated by what we see reflected about ourselves in the eyes of other people. It is only when others respect us that we respect ourselves. It is only when others love us that we love ourselves. It is only when others find us pleasant and desirable and worthy that we come to terms with our own egos. Occasionally, a person is created with such towering self-confidence that he doesn't seem to need the acceptance of other people, but he is indeed a rare bird. The vast majority of us are dependent on our associates for emotional sustenance each day. What does this say, then, about those who exist in a state of perpetual isolation, being deprived of loving, caring human contact year after year? Such people are virtually certain to experience feelings of worthlessness and its stepchildren, deep depression and despair.

Why do housewives, particularly, allow themselves to be sealed off from meaningful friendships and associations outside their homes? Why does their natural course seem to take them toward further loneliness and emotional deprival? I believe there are at least six explanations for the isolation of women, today, and I think we should examine each of them briefly.

1. Small children isolate a mother. It's such a hassle to pack the porta-crib and the diapers and all the supportive paraphernalia in the car, and go off to visit a friend. Mom has to wonder if it's worth the effort. Then too, the kids won't play by themselves and they keep the women from enjoying the occasion, anyway. And if the youngsters are not well disciplined, their mother is embarrassed to take them anywhere and the invitations

become more scarce from her former friends who simply can't stand to have her brats in their houses. Thus, the mothers of preschool children often give up and stay at home, spending month after month predominantly in the company of "little people." I heard of one such mother who was finally given an opportunity to get out of the house. Her husband's company had prepared a banquet in honor of retiring employees, and she was seated beside the president himself. She was very nervous about talking to a real, live adult again. She feared she might revert to baby talk during the course of the evening. To her surprise, however, she conversed without a flaw through the entire meal, speaking of world events and current political conditions. Then she realized with dismay that throughout their conversation, she had been dutifully cutting the president's meat and wiping his mouth with her napkin. I suppose you could call this a housewife's occupational hazard.

2. Though avant garde feminists may chew me to pieces for saying so, it is my observation that women can be absolutely vicious with each other. Having supervised female employees through the years, I have stood in amazement as they scratched and clawed one another over the most minor conflicts. One explosion of monumental consequence began with a disagreement among four secretaries about which deodorant was the most effective! Can you imagine four red-faced women screaming at each other over whether to spray it or roll it on?! (The "real" conflict, of course, involved resentment having nothing to do with deodorant.) I have employed two or three particularly talented antagonists who could stir up more trouble in an afternoon than I could untangle in a week. But this same competitiveness and suspicion is also represented among housewives, I believe. There are many women who simply can't stand other women. There are other less aggressive individuals who are greatly threatened by their feminine associates. Such a woman

wouldn't think of inviting "the girls" over for tea unless she had spit-shined her house inside and out, and prepared a super-delicious dessert. And those who have nicer homes will never be invited to the cottages of women who are embarrassed by their humble dwellings. And those whose husbands have professional, higher-paying jobs are often deeply resented by those who must struggle to pay the utility bills each month. In summary, women are often pitted against the very people whom they need for mutual respect and acceptance. The result is loneliness and boredom.

3. Feelings of inferiority, themselves, serve to isolate women (and men) from each other. I have already stated the converse: isolation increases inferiority. These two conditions often interact in a vicious cycle, spiraling ever downward into despair and loneliness. The woman who has no friends—and I mean no "real" friends—feels too inferior to make new social contacts, and her failure to make friends makes her feel even more inferior. A housewife in this predicament is a prime candidate for "secret" alcoholism or drug abuse, or even suicide. She is desperate for meaningful contact with people, yet her behavior is often misinterpreted by her peers as being "stuck up," cold, aloof or self-sufficient.

4. Women are often less successful in finding outside interests and activities than are their masculine counterparts. Men typically love sporting events, and draw great enthusiasm from following the (televised) games of the home team. Women do not. Men usually like to hunt and fish and hike in the wilderness. Women stay home and wait for them. Men like to bowl and play golf and tennis and basketball and softball. Women watch while yawning on the sidelines. Men like to build and fix things, and work in the garage. Women remain inside washing the dishes. Men find recreation in boating and auto racing and everything mechanical. Women are bored with such nonsense. Now obviously, these are generalizations which

have innumerable exceptions, but the fact remains that men usually lack the time to pursue all their varied interests, while their wives may find it difficult to generate much genuine enthusiasm for anything. I suspect that the cultural influences of early childhood stamp a certain passivity on little girls, constricting their field of interests. For whatever reasons, the world of women is typically more narrow than that of men. For proof of this fact, listen to the conversations of the women as opposed to men at your next social gathering. The feminine discussion will probably center around children, cosmetics, and other people's behavior; the men will talk about a much greater variety of topics. It should not be surprising then, that boredom ranks high as a source of depression among women.

5. Fatigue and time pressure, discussed in the last chapter, must also serve to isolate the mothers of small children. There simply isn't enough time and energy to open the door to the outside world.

6. Financial limitations in an inflationary economy certainly restrict the activities of housewives. We will discuss these problems in a subsequent chapter.

Certainly, there are many reasons why housewives can find themselves lonely, isolated, and bored, even if they live in the midst of six million other lonely people. And what agitation is caused by their emptiness. One writer said, "Everybody must be somebody to somebody to be anybody!" I agree. A lyricist expressed a similar concept in his song entitled, "You're Nobody till Somebody Loves You." Dr. William Glasser explained this same psychological principle in his popular text *Reality Therapy*: "At all times in our lives we must have at least one person who cares about us and whom we care for ourselves. If we do not have this essential person, we will not be able to fulfill our basic needs." Obviously, we human beings are social animals and must continually depend on each other for emotional stability.

Emotional Differences Between Men and Women

At this point I offer a message of great importance to every husband who loves and wants to understand his wife. Whereas men and women have the same needs for self-worth and belonging, they typically satisfy those needs differently. A man derives his sense of worth primarily from the reputation he earns in his job or profession. He draws emotional satisfaction from achieving in business, becoming financially independent, developing a highly respected craft or skill, supervising others, becoming "boss," or by being loved and appreciated by his patients or clients or fellow businessmen. The man who is successful in these areas does not depend on his wife as his *primary* shield against inferiority. Of course, she plays an important role as his companion and lover, but she isn't essential to his self-respect day by day.

By contrast, a housewife approaches her marriage from a totally different perspective. She does not have access to "other" sources of self-esteem commonly available to her husband. She can cook a good dinner, but once it is eaten her family may not even remember to thank her for it. Her household duties do not bring her respect in the community, and she is not likely to be praised for the quality of her dusting techniques. Therefore, the more isolated she becomes, as we have discussed, the more vital her man will be to her sense of fulfillment, confidence, and well-being. He must be that "one person" of whom Dr. Glasser wrote, and if he is not, she is "unable to fulfill her basic needs." That spells trouble with a capital T.

Let's reduce it to a useful oversimplification: men derive self-esteem by being *respected;* women feel worthy when they are *loved.* This may be the most important personality distinction between the sexes.

This understanding helps explain the unique views of marriage as seen by men and women. A man can be contented with a kind of business partnership in marriage, provided sexual privileges are part of the arrangement. As long as his wife prepares his dinner each evening, is reasonably amiable, and doesn't nag him during football season, he can be satisfied. The romantic element is nice—but not necessary. However, this kind of surface relationship drives his wife utterly wild with frustration. She must have something more meaningful. Women yearn to be the special sweethearts of their men, being repected and appreciated and loved with tenderness. This is why a housewife often thinks about her husband during the day and eagerly awaits his arrival home; it explains why their wedding anniversary is more important to her, and why he gets clobbered when he forgets it. It explains why she is constantly "reaching" for him when he is at home, trying to pull him out of the newspaper or television set; it explains why *Absence of Romantic Love in My Marriage* ranked so high as a source of depression among women, whereas men would have rated it somewhere in the vicinity of last place.

As stated in the early pages of this book, women often find it impossible to convey their needs for romantic affection to their husbands. One fellow listened carefully as I explained the frustration his wife had expressed to me; he promptly went out and bought some flowers for her and rang the front doorbell. When she opened the door, he extended his arm and said, "Here!" Having met his marital responsibilities, he pushed past her and turned on the television set. His wife was not exactly overwhelmed by his generosity.

Another man said, "I just don't understand my wife. She has everything she could possibly want. She has a dishwasher and a new dryer, and we live in a nice neighborhood. I don't drink or beat the kids or kick the dog. I've been faithful since the day we were married. But she's miserable and I can't figure out why!" His love-starved wife would have traded the dishwasher, the dryer, and the dog for a single expression of genuine tenderness from her unromantic husband. Appliances do not build self-esteem; being somebody's sweetheart most certainly does.

Instead of building confidence and preserving romantic excitement, many men seem determined to do the opposite, particularly in public. Have you ever watched a person (usually a man) play the popular game called "Assassinate the Spouse?" Any number of couples can play this destructive game, and its objective is simple: each contestant attempts to punish his mate by ridiculing and embarrassing her in front of their friends. Although he can hurt her verbally when they are alone, he can cut her to pieces when onlookers are present. And if he wants to be especially vicious, he lets the guests know he thinks she is dumb and ugly; those are the two places where she is most vulnerable. Bonus points are awarded if he can reduce her to tears.

Why would anyone want to publicize his (or her) resentment in this manner? The reason is that hostility seeks its own ventilation, and most angry people find their feelings difficult to contain. But how unfortunate is the couple who slug it out before spectators. This brutal game has no winners; the contest ends when one player is totally divested of his self-respect and dignity.

I have often wished there were an acceptable method for men and women to ventilate their feelings in private. A golfer can pound the ball around an eighteen-hole course, and somehow feel more tranquil in the clubhouse. Weekend basketball players throw their elbows at each other in the gymnasium and thereby reduce their frustrations and tensions. Professional hockey players unload their anxieties by smashing their opponents with their sticks and skates. Unfortunately, however, there is no convenient method for husbands and wives to work out their hostilities. They can only glare at each other in silence across a room. I have given considerable thought to this problem and believe I have a workable solution. I am proposing that every well-designed home of the future be equipped with a bumper car rink—the kind that is found at all state fairgrounds and amusement parks. If you've ever watched the drivers of these vehicles smashing each other at full speed, you've seen their dilated eyes and the wicked grins on their faces. They bellow with delight when they catch an unsuspecting driver broadside, knocking his car across the rink. Wouldn't it be great if a husband and wife could schedule one hour a day, probably from 5 to 6 P.M., on a bumper car track? I can hear them muttering as they smash each others' cars: "Hah! That's what you get for being so stingy with our money!" or "Take that!" (Wham!) "That'll teach you to be so grouchy when you come home." After fifty hits each, a bell would ring, signaling the end of the hour, and the two "cleansed" drivers would emerge as lovely friends for the remainder of the evening. Do you suppose the world is ready for this remedy just yet?

The 5000-Year-Old Solution

There is still no substitute for the biblical prescription for marriage, nor will its wisdom ever be replaced. A successful husband and wife relationship begins with the attitude of the man; he has been ordained by God as the head of the family, and the responsibility for its welfare rests upon his shoulders. This charge can be found in the early writings of Moses in the Old Testament, returning at least 5000 years into Jewish history. Deuteronomy 24:5 (TLB) reads:

A newly married man is not to be drafted into the army nor given any other responsibilities; for a year he shall be free to be at home, happy with his wife.

Imagine the luxury! Newlyweds were given one full year in which to adjust to married life, with no responsibilities or duties during that period. (I must admit that I don't know what they did with their time after the first three weeks, but it sounds like fun, anyway.) Compare it with the first year of marriage in this day, when the man and woman are both working, going to school, and all too frequently the bride is facing the biological, emotional, and financial tensions of a pregnancy. But my point in quoting this Scripture is better illustrated by the last sentence as stated in the King James version. It reads, "And he (the husband) shall *cheer up* his wife which he hath taken."

Early Mosaic law made it clear that the emotional well-being of a wife is the specific responsibility of her husband. It was his job to "cheer" her. Friends and neighbors, it still is! This message is for the man whose own ego needs have drawn him to achieve super success in life, working seven days a week and consuming himself in a continual quest for power and status. If his wife and children do not fit into his schedule somewhere, he deserves the conflict that is certainly coming. This masculine charge should also be heeded by the husband who hoards his nonworking hours for his own pleasures, fishing every weekend, burying his head in the television set, or living on a golf course. Everyone needs recreation and these activities have an important reconstructive role to play. But when our enjoyment begins to suffocate those who need us—those whose very existence depends on our commitment—it has gone too far and requires regulation.

Derek Prince has expressed this viewpoint even more strongly. He feels that the troubles America is facing, particularly with reference to the family, can be traced to what he calls "renegade males." The word renegade actually means "one who has reneged." We men have ignored our God-given responsibility to care for the welfare of our families, to discipline our children, to supervise the expenditure of the financial resources, to assume spiritual leadership, to love and to cherish and protect. Instead, we have launched ourselves on a lifetime ego trip, thinking only of our needs and our pleasures and our status. Is it any wonder that low self-esteem is a problem among our women? Is it surprising that loneliness, isolation, and boredom have reached critical proportions? Both these canyons of depression are dug by the deterioration of relationships between husbands and wives, and we men are in the best position to improve the situation.

Am I recommending that men dominate their wives, ruling with an iron fist and robbing them of individuality? Certainly not. Again, the prescription for a successful marriage is found in the Bible, where the concept of the family originated. God, who created the entire universe, should be able to tell us how to live together harmoniously. He has done just that, as written in Ephesians 5:28-33 (TLB).

That is how husbands should treat their wives, loving them as part of themselves. For since a man and his wife are now one, a man is really doing himself a favor and loving himself when he loves his wife! No one hates his own body but lovingly cares for it, just as Christ cares for his body the Church, of which we are parts. (That the husband and wife are one body is proved by the Scripture which says, 'A man must leave his father and mother when he marries, so that he can be perfectly joined to his wife, and the two shall be one!') I know this is hard to understand, but it is an illustration of the way we are parts of the body of Christ. So again I say, a man must love his wife as a part of himself; and the wife must see to it that she deeply respects her husband, obeying, praising, and honoring him.

There is certainly no room for masculine oppression within that formula. The husband is charged with loving leadership within the family, but he must recognize his wife's feelings and needs as being one with his own. When she hurts, he hurts, and takes steps to end the pain. What she wants, he wants, and satisfies her needs. And through all this, his wife deeply respects, praises and even obeys her loving husband. If this one prescription were applied within the American family, we would have little need for divorce courts, alimony, visiting rights, crushed children, broken hearts, and shattered lives.

Now, if we appear to be blaming all marital and family woes on husbands, let me clarify the point. For every complaint women have against men, there is a corresponding bellyache on the other end of the line. And I'm certain that I've heard them all. Women can be just as selfish and irresponsible as their men. How many wives have "let themselves go," waddling around on massive rhino haunches and looking like they had spent the night in a tornado? How many husbands come home every night to a wrecked house, dirty kids, and a nagging, groaning, overindulged wife? King Solomon must have known such a sweetheart, for he wrote:

> It is better to live in the corner of an attic than with a crabby woman in a lovely home (Proverbs 21:9, TLB).

Neither sex has a monopoly on offensive behavior.

But for those who accept God's design for the family, it is clear that husbands bear the *initial* responsibility for correcting the problem. This obligation is implicit in the role of leadership assigned to males. Where does it begin? By men treating their wives with the same dignity and attention that they give to their own bodies, "loving them even as Christ loved the Church, giving his life for it." What a challenge! If this be male chauvinism, then may the whole masculine world be swept by its philosophy.

Would it be ostentatious for me to give a personal illustration at this point? I hope not, and ask that the reader not interpret this statement as boasting. My wife, Shirley, and I have applied the biblical prescription in our own marriage, and have found it valid and true. Having been with Shirley daily since we were married fourteen years ago, I still enjoy the pleasure of her company. In fact, if I could choose anyone on earth with whom to spend a free evening, Shirley would rank at the top of the list. She feels the same way about me, which is even more remarkable! I suppose it can be summarized this way: Shirley and I are not just married to one another; we are also "best friends." Does this mean that we never have strong differences of opinion? Certainly not. Does it mean that we float along on a pink cloud of adolescent romanticism every day of our lives? No chance. Does it mean that irritability and other human frailties have been conquered? Not likely. Perhaps I should tell you about our one absolutely unresolvable problem; there is an area of difficulty between us which defies correction or mediation, and I have even lost hope of ever coming to terms with it: Shirley and I operate on totally different thermostats. Even though we have become "one body" we have vastly differing ideas of how hot it should be! My wife is cold at least eleven months out of the year, thawing momentarily during the summer. She warmed up last August 14 for about an hour, right around noon, and then froze over again. Wouldn't you know that I stay overheated the year around, and gasp for a cool breeze in the California sunshine. This differing viewpoint produces some dramatic struggles for control of the heating unit in our home. A man's home is his castle they say, but in my case, it's a furnace.

Obviously, the success of my relationship with Shirley

does not result from human perfection on either part. It is simply a product of caring for the feelings, needs, and concerns of the other. It is giving, not grabbing. Or as it is stated in the marriage vows, "In honor, preferring one another." And by some strange quirk of human nature, that attitude produces self-esteem by the bushel.

A Closer Look at Reality

Having described the domestic responsibilities of husbands and fathers in graphic detail, we are now *obligated* to consider some very thorny questions which perplex the wives of men who haven't been listening. Let's face it, only 20 percent of the readers of this kind of book are likely to be men. Therefore, we cannot ignore the plight of the woman whose husband "ought to" but doesn't. What should be her attitude if he is continually unsympathetic to her emotional needs and longings? What if he refuses to accept his designated role as the loving, caring leader of the family? How should a wife cope with emotional abandonment, playing second fiddle to his job, or televised sports, or a consuming hobby, or even another woman? It would be almost unethical for me to write on the subject of depression in women without confronting these issues head-on, for if my observations are accurate, *most* women have sought to answer those lingering questions for themselves.

Before offering my views on this subject, however, let's pause to examine the suggestions of others. Let's suppose that a lonely, discouraged wife visits her local bookstore to seek advice and counsel in the writings of the "experts." Assuming that the most popular books would probably provide the greatest help, she examines the more prominently displayed volumes in the marriage and family section of the store. The first text that she considers is entitled *Open Marriage,* which proclaims itself to be the Number One Bestseller in America. If she buys and reads it, she will learn that marriage is far healthier when swinging husbands and wives keep a little hanky-panky going on the side. Get the message, now! A man and woman, so the authors say, will be inexorably drawn together by knowing that their mate may be sleeping with someone new tomorrow night. Can't you visualize Jack coming home at 6:00 A.M. for breakfast, and his wife says, "Where have you been, honey?"

"Oh," he replied, "I slept with Janice last night and I'm sure tired."

"Well," responds his sympathetic wife, "I hope you won't be too worn out to babysit tonight, 'cause I'll be spending the night with Paul."

Ridiculous? Sure, but *Open Marriage* has sold a million copies to desperate and gullible readers. Moreover, the misguided writers of this unfortunate book have now become great authorities on family harmony, no less.

Here's how Judith Viorst sees *Open Marriage,* as quoted from her article, "Just Because I'm Married Does It Mean I'm Going Steady?" in *Redbook* magazine, dated May 1973:

> So why can't a husband go skiing with some other woman? Why can't a wife see a movie with some other man? Why can't a man have women for friends even after he's married? Why can't married women have friendships with men?
>
> I think I've got an answer to those questions, but maybe all I've got is a dirty mind. I've also got some statements (from Nena and George O'Neill's book *Open Marriage*) on the benefits of the broadminded point of view.
>
> Frank: "If Janet goes out of an evening, I want her to have a good time, to have an interesting time. She shares her experiences with me and I gain enrichment in my life . . ."
>
> (I can see it now. "Wake up, Milton," I'll say.

"Sorry I'm so late, but you know how fascinating Arnie is. And wait until I tell you this incredible story he told me—it'll enrich your life.")

Another happy husband told the O'Neills: "It's a great feeling to walk down the street . . . and know that if I meet someone, male or female, that I want to know, I can do it without feeling guilty—we can have a drink, take advantage of the spontaneity of the moment—and I don't have to worry about how I'm going to explain it all when I get home."

Well, he's lucky he isn't married to someone like me, because, let me guarantee you, he'd *have* to feel guilty. And explain it all. Especially the part that goes "take advantage of the spontaneity of the moment."

But mine, the O'Neills would point out, is—alas!—a closed marriage, which augurs ill for my future married life. The grass, they say, is greener on the other side of the fence only when you've bothered building fences. Lead us not into temptation, I say back.[1]

Sitting beside *Open Marriage* on the top shelf is another bestseller which would tell our depressed friend to sabotage her marriage altogether. It is entitled *Creative Divorce,* and proposes some innovative concepts, among them, "Divorce is not the end . . . it is the beginning. Make it work for you," and "To say goodbye is to say hello. Hello to a new life . . . to a new freer, more self-assured you. Hello to new ways of looking at the world and of relating to people. Your divorce can be the very best thing that ever happened to you!" How's that for an original approach to family life? Kick the bum out of the house and giggle your way into a world of continual delight and bliss. If our housewife is given this irresponsible suggestion at the precise moment of her greatest despair, she may turn her sick marriage into a dead one. Every physician knows that it is easy to kill his patient;

the skill comes in curing him. Yet in *Creative Divorce*, the "patient" is told to ignore all other medications and remedies that might restore the health and vitality of his family life. I wish I knew how many marriages this single book has destroyed.

The bombardment of irresponsible and damnable solutions to emotional isolation are seemingly endless at this time in our history. If a concept is audacious and anti-Christian, you can bet that someone with professional degrees and credentials has recommended it during the past two decades. And he's probably sold it by the barrel to a confused and morally bankrupt populace. We have heard the noted anthropologist, Dr. Margaret Mead, advocate trial marriage for the young; we have been propagandized to accept communal marriage and contract marriage and cohabitation. Even our music has reflected our aimless groping for an innovative relationship between men and women. One such idea is that romantic love can survive only in the *absence* of permanent commitment. Singer Glen Campbell translated this thought into music in his popular song entitled "Gentle on My Mind." I'll paraphrase the lyrics: He said it was not the ink-stained signatures dried on some marriage certificate that kept his bedroll stashed behind the couch in his lover's home; it was knowing that he could get up and leave her anytime he wished—that she had no hooks into his hide. It was the freedom to abandon her that kept her "gentle on (his) mind." What a foolish notion. How utterly crass to think such a woman exists who could let her lover come and go with no feelings of loss, rejection, or abandonment. How ignorant it is of the power of love (and sex) to make us "one flesh" . . . inevitably ripping and tearing that flesh at the time of separation. And, of course, Brother Campbell's song said nothing about the little children who are born from such a relationship, each one wondering if daddy will be there tomorrow morning . . . if he will help them pay their bills

75

. . . or if he'll be out by a railroad track somewhere, sipping coffee from a tin can and thinking the good thoughts in the backroads of his mind. Can't you see his little woman standing with her children in the front doorway, waving a hanky and calling, "Goodbye, dear. Drop in when you can." Despite the stupidity of this message, "Gentle on My Mind" reached the top of the record charts, purchased blindly by those who believe that uncommitted love offers a viable alternative to marriage.

Obviously, the irresponsible, destructive "solutions" to knotty problems are not difficult to generate. They have always been easier to develop than those which provide a way out of the mire. Admittedly, I don't possess every answer to the problems I have posed. I know of no magical tricks that will turn a cold, unresponsive man into a compassionate, communicative, romantic dream machine. But I can offer some suggestions which I have found to be helpful in my counseling experience.

First, a woman who wants to reignite the romantic fires in her husband must look for ways to *teach* him about her needs. As I have attempted to explain, men have different emotional needs than women, making it hard for them to comprehend the feelings and longings of their wives. To correct this lack of understanding, women often resort to nagging, pleading, scolding, complaining and accusing. This is how it sounds to an exhausted man who has come home from work moments before: "Won't you just put down that newspaper, George, and give me five minutes of your time? Five minutes—is that too much to ask? You never seem to care about my feelings, anyway. How long has it been since we went out for dinner? Even if we did, you'd probably take the newspaper along with you. I'll tell you, George, sometimes I think you don't care about me and the kids anymore. If just once . . . just once . . . you would show a little love and understanding, I would drop dead from sheer shock, etc., etc., etc."

I hope my feminine readers know that this verbal barrage at the end of a work day is *not* what I mean by teaching. It's like pounding George behind the ear with a two-by-four, and it rarely achieves more than a snarl when he gets up from the floor. Nagging shuts down communication with amazing efficiency. By contrast, teaching is a matter of timing, setting and manner.

1. Timing

Select the moment when your husband is typically more responsive and pleasant; perhaps that opportunity will occur immediately after the evening meal, or when the light goes out at night, or in the freshness of the morning. The worst time of the day is during the first sixty minutes after he arrives home from work, yet this is the usual combat hour. Don't lumber into such a heavy debate without giving it proper planning and forethought, taking advantage of every opportunity for the success of the effort.

2. Setting

The ideal situation is to ask your husband to take you on an overnight or weekend trip to a pleasant area. If financial considerations will cause him to decline, save the money out of household funds or other resources. If it is impossible to get away, the next best alternative is to obtain a babysitter and go out to breakfast or dinner alone. If that too is out of the question, then select a time at home when the children are occupied and the phone can be taken off the hook. Generally speaking, however, the farther you can get him from home, with its cares and problems and stresses, the better will be your chance to achieve genuine communication.

3. Manner

It is extremely important that your husband does not view your conversation as a personal attack. We are all equipped with emotional defenses which rise to our aid when we are being vilified. Don't trigger those defensive mechanisms. Instead, your manner should be as warm, loving, and supportive as possible under the circumstances. Let it be known that you are attempting to interpret *your* needs and desires, not *his* inadequacies and shortcomings. Furthermore, you must take his emotional state into consideration, as well. Postpone the conversation if he is under unusual stress from his work, or if he isn't feeling well, or if he has recently been stung by circumstances and events. Then when the timing, setting, and manner converge to produce a moment of opportunity, express your deep feelings as effectively as possible. Use the earlier sections of this book for ammunition, and like every good boy scout: be *prepared*.

Of course, one conversation is rarely sufficient to produce a long-term change in behavior and attitude. The woman who wants to be understood will continually teach her husband about her feelings and desires, while doing her best to meet his unique needs.

Am I suggesting that a woman should crawl on her belly like a subservient puppy, begging her master for a pat on the head? Certainly not! It is of the highest priority to maintain a distinct element of dignity and self-respect *throughout* the husband-wife relationship. This takes us into a related area that requires the greatest emphasis. I have observed that many (if not most) marriages suffer from a failure to recognize a universal characteristic of human nature. *We value that which we are fortunate to get; we discredit that with which we are stuck! We lust for the very thing which is beyond our grasp; we disdain that same item when it becomes a permanent possession.* No toy is ever as much fun to play with as it appeared to a wide-eyed child in a store. Seldom does an expensive automobile provide the satisfaction anticipated by the man who dreamed of its ownership. This principle is even more dramatically accurate in romantic affairs, particularly with reference to men. Let's look at the extreme case of a Don Juan, the perpetual lover who romps from one feminine flower to another. His heart throbs and pants after the elusive princess who drops her glass slipper as she flees. Every ounce of energy is focused on her capture. However, the intensity of his desire is dependent on her unavailability. The moment his passionate dreams materialize, he begins to ask himself, "Is this what I really want?" Farther down the line as the relationship progresses toward the routine circumstances of everyday life, he is attracted by new princesses and begins to wonder how he can escape the older model.

Now, I would not imply that all men, or even the majority of them, are as exploitative and impermanent as the gadabout I described. But to a lesser degree, most men *and* women are impelled by the same urges. How many times have I seen a bored, tired relationship become a torrent of desire and longing the moment one partner rejects the other and walks out. After years of apathy, the "dumpee" suddenly burns with romantic desire and desperate hope.

This principle hits even closer to home for me at this moment. Right now, as I am writing these words, I am sitting in the waiting room of a large hospital while my wife is undergoing major, abdominal surgery. I am writing to ease my tension and anxiety. While I have always been close to Shirley, my appreciation and tender love for her are maximal this morning. Less than five minutes ago, a surgeon emerged from the operating room with a grim face, informing the man near me that his wife is consumed with cancer. He spoke in unguarded terms of the unfavorable pathological report and the malignant infestation. I will be speaking to Shirley's surgeon within the hour and my vulnerability is keenly felt. While my love for my wife has *never* flagged through our fourteen years together, it has rarely been as intense as in this moment of threat. You see, not only are our emotions affected by the challenge of pursuit, but also by the possibility of irrevocable loss. (The surgeon arrived as I was writing the sentence above, saying my wife came through the operation with no complications, and the pathologist recognized no abnormal tissue. I am indeed a grateful man! My deepest sympathy is with the less fortunate family whose tragedy I witnessed today.)

A better example of fickle emotions is illustrated by my early relationship with Shirley. When we first met, she was a lowly sophomore in college and I was a lofty senior. I viewed myself as a big man on campus, and my relationship with this young coed mattered little to me. She, in turn, had been very successful with boys, and was greatly challenged by the independence I demonstrated. She wanted to win me primarily because she wasn't sure she could . . . but her enthusiasm inhibited my own interest in return. After graduation, we had one of those lengthy conversations well known to lovers the world over, when I said I wanted her to date other fellows while I was in the Army, because I didn't plan to get married soon. I'll never forget her reaction. I expected Shirley to cry and hold on to me. Instead, she said, "I've been thinking the same thoughts, and I *would* like to date other guys. Why don't we just go our separate ways, for now." Her answer rocked me. For the first time in our relationship, she was moving away from me. What I didn't know was that Shirley stoically closed her front door and then cried all night.

I went away to the Army and returned to a nearby school (the University of Southern California) for my graduate training. By this time, Shirley was an exalted senior and I was a collegiate has-been. She was homecoming queen, senior class president, a member of *Who's Who in American Colleges and Universities,* and one of the most popular girls in her class. And as might be expected, she suddenly looked very attractive to me. I began to call several times a day, complain about who she was spending her time with, and try to find ways to please my dream girl. However, the moment Shirley saw my enthusiasm and anxiety, her affection began to die. Gone was the challenge which had attracted her two years before. Instead, I had become just another fellow pounding on her door and asking for favors.

One day after a particularly uninspiring date, I sat down at a desk and spent two solid hours thinking about what was happening. And during the course of that introspection, I realized the mistake I was making. A light flashed in my head and I grabbed a pen and wrote ten changes I was going to make in our relationship. First, I was determined to demonstrate self-respect and dignity, even if I lost the one I now loved so deeply. Secondly, I decided to convey this attitude every time I got the chance: "I am going somewhere in life, and I'm anxious to get there. I love you, and hope you choose to go with me. If you do, I'll give myself to you and try to make you happy. However, if you choose not to make the journey with me, then I can't force my will on you. The decision is yours, and I'll accept it." There were other elements to my new manner, but they all centered around self-confidence and independence.

The first night when I applied the new formula was one of the most thrilling experiences of my life. The girl who is now my wife saw me starting to slip away on that evening, and she reacted with alarm. We were riding in silence in my car, and Shirley asked me to pull over to the curb and stop. When I did she put her arms around my neck and said, "I'm afraid I'm losing you and I don't know why. Do you still love me?" I noticed by the reflected light of the moon that she had tears in her eyes. She obviously didn't hear my thumping heart as I made a little speech about my solitary journey in life. You see, I had reestablished the challenge for Shirley, and she responded beautifully.

The psychological force which produced our see-saw relationship is an important one, since it is almost universal in human nature. Forgive the redundancy, but I must restate the principle: *we crave that which we can't attain, but we disrespect that which we can't escape.* This axiom is particularly relevant in romantic matters, and has probably influenced *your* love life, too. Now, the forgotten part of this characteristic is that marriage does not erase or change it. Whenever one marriage partner grovels in his own disrespect . . . when he reveals his fear of rejection by his mate . . . when he begs and pleads for a handout . . . he often faces a bewildering attitude of disdain from the one he needs and loves. Just as in the premarital relationship, nothing douses more water on a romantic flame than for one partner to fling himself emotionally on the other, accepting disrespect in stride. He says in effect, "No matter how badly you treat me, I'll still be here at your feet, because I can't survive without you." That is the best way I know to kill a beautiful friendship.

So what am I recommending . . . that husbands and wives scratch and claw each other to show their independence? No! That they play a sneaky cat and mouse game to recreate a "challenge"? Not at all! I am merely suggesting that self-respect and dignity be maintained in the relationship. Let's look at a case in point.

Suppose that one partner, the husband, begins to show signs of disinterest in his wife. Let's say that their sex life has been rather dull lately, and the sense of emotional togetherness is more of a memory than a reality. (The decline of a marriage is rarely brought about by a blowout; it's usually a slow leak.) Then the relationship reaches a low point and the husband consistently treats his wife rudely and disrespectfully in public, pulling behind a wall of silence when they are at home. These are symptoms of a condition which I call "the trapped syndrome." More often than not, the man is thinking these kinds of thoughts: "I'm 35 years old" (or whatever age) "and I'm not getting any younger. Do I really want to spend the rest of my life with this one woman? I'm bored with her and there are others who interest me more. But there's no way out 'cause I'm stuck." These are the feelings which usually precede esoteric infidelity, and they certainly can be felt in the strain between a husband and wife.

How should a woman respond when she reads the cues and realizes that her husband feels trapped? Obviously, the worst thing she could do is reinforce the cage around him, yet that is likely to be her initial reaction. As she thinks about how important he is to her, and what-on-earth she would do without him, and whether he's involved with another woman, her anxiety may compel her to grab and hold him. Her begging and pleading only drive him to disrespect her more, and the relationship continues to splinter. There is a better way which I have found productive in counseling experience. The most successful approach to bringing a partner back toward the center of a relationship is not to follow when he moves away from it. Instead of saying, "Why do you do me this way?" and "Why won't you talk to me?" and "Why don't you care anymore?" a wife should pull back a few inches herself. When she passes her husband in the hall and would ordinarily touch him or seek his attention, she should move by him without notice. Silence by him is greeted by silence in return. She should not be hostile or aggressive, ready to explode when he finally asks her to say what is on her mind. Rather, she responds in kind . . . being quietly confident, independent and mysterious. The effect of this behavior is to open the door on his trap. Instead of clamping herself to his neck like a blood-sucking leech, she releases her grip and introduces a certain challenge in his mind, as well. He may begin to wonder if he has gone too far and may be losing something precious to him. If that will not turn him around, then the relationship is stone, cold dead.

The message I have attempted to convey is extremely difficult to express in written form, and I am certain to be misinterpreted by some of my readers on this issue. I haven't suggested that women rise up in anger—that they stamp their feet and demand their domestic rights, or that they sulk and pout in silence. Please do not associate me with those contemporary voices which are mobilizing feminine troops for all-out sexual combat. Nothing is less attractive to me than an angry woman who is determined to grab her share, one way or the other. No, the answer is not found in hostile aggression, but in quiet self-respect!

In short, personal dignity in a marriage is maintained the same way it was produced during the dating days. The attitude should be, "I love you and am totally committed to you, but I only control my half of the relationship. I can't demand your love in return. You came to me of your free will when we agreed to marry. No one forced us together. That same free will is necessary to keep our love alive. If you choose to walk away from me, I will be crushed and hurt beyond description, because I have withheld nothing of myself. Nevertheless, I will let you go and ultimately I will survive. I couldn't demand your affection in the beginning, and I can only request it now."

Returning to the recommendation that a woman "teach" her husband about her needs, it can be done within the atmosphere of self-respect that I have described. In fact, it *must* be handled in that manner.

The Meaning of Love

It has been of concern to me that many young people grow up with a very distorted concept of romantic love. They are taught to confuse the real thing with infatuation and to idealize marriage into something it can never be. To help remedy this situation, I developed a brief true or false test for use in teaching groups of teen-agers. But to my surprise, I found that adults do not score much higher on the quiz than their adolescent offspring. The ten-item test is reproduced below for those who would like to measure their understanding of romantic love:

Beliefs about Love—a Self Quiz

Please circle the correct answer, true or false

1. I believe "love at first sight" occurs between some people.   True   False
2. I believe it is easy to distinguish real love from infatuation.   True   False
3. I believe people who sincerely love each other will not fight and argue.   True   False
4. I believe God selects *one* particular person for each of us to marry, and he will guide us together.   True   False
5. I believe if a man and woman genuinely love each other, then hardships and troubles will have little or no effect on their relationship.   True   False
6. I believe it is better to marry the wrong person than to remain single and lonely throughout life.   True   False
7. I believe it is not harmful to have sexual intercourse before marriage if the couple has a meaningful relationship.   True   False
8. I believe if a couple is genuinely in love, that condition is permanent—lasting a lifetime.   True   False
9. I believe short courtships (six months or less) are best.   True   False
10. I believe teen-agers are more capable of genuine love than are older people.   True   False

While there are undoubtedly some differences of opinion regarding the answers for this quiz, I feel strongly about what I consider to be correct responses to each item. In fact, I believe many of the common marital hang-ups develop from a misunderstanding of these ten issues. The confusion begins when boy meets girl and the entire sky lights up in romantic profusion. Smoke and fire are followed by lightning and thunder, and alas, two trembly-voiced adolescents find themselves knee deep in true love. Adrenalin and sixty-four other hormones are dumped into the cardio-vascular system by the pint, and every nerve is charged with 110 volts of electricity. Then two little fellows go racing up the respective backbones and blast their exhilarating message into each spinning head: "This is it! The search is over! You've found the perfect human being! Hooray for love!"

For our romantic young couple, it is simply too wonderful to behold. They want to be together twenty-four hours a day . . . to take walks in the rain and sit by the fire and kiss and munch and cuddle. They get all choked up just thinking about each other. And it doesn't take long for the subject of marriage to arise. So they set the date and reserve the chapel and contact the minister and order the flowers. The big night arrives, amidst mother's tears and dad's grins and jealous bridesmaids and bratty little flower-girls. The candles are lit and two beautiful songs are butchered by the bride's sister. Then the vows are muttered and the rings are placed on trembling fingers, and the preacher tells the groom to kiss his new wife. Then they sprint up the aisle, each flashing thirty-two teeth, on the way to the reception room. Their friends and well-wishers hug and kiss the bride and roll their eyes at the groom, and eat the awful cake and follow the instructions of the perspiring photographer. Finally, the new Mr. and Mrs. run from the church in a flurry of rice and confetti and strike out on their honeymoon. So far the beautiful dream remains intact, but it is living on borrowed time.

The first night in the motel is not only less exciting than

advertised . . . it turns into a comical disaster. She is exhausted and tense and he is self-conscious and phony. From the beginning, sex is tinged with the threat of possible failure. Their vast expectations about the marital bed lead to disappointment and frustration and fear. Since most human beings have a neurotic desire to feel sexually adequate, each partner tends to blame his mate for their orgasmic problems, which will eventually add a note of anger and resentment to their relationship.

About three o'clock on the second afternoon, he gives ten minutes serious thought to the fateful question, "Have I made an enormous mistake?" His silence increases her anxieties, and the seeds of disenchantment are born. Each partner has far too much time to think about the consequences of this new relationship, and they both begin to feel trapped.

Their initial argument is a silly thing; they struggle momentarily over how much money to spend for dinner on the third night of the honeymoon. She wants to go someplace romantic to charge up the atmosphere, and he wants to eat with Ronald McDonald. The flare-up only lasts a few moments and is followed by apologies, but some harsh words have been exchanged which took the keen edge off the beautiful dream. They will soon learn to hurt each other more effectively.

Somehow, they make it through the six-day trip and drive home to set up house together. Then the world starts to splinter and disentegrate before their eyes. The next fight is bigger and better than the first; he leaves home for two hours and she calls her mother. Throughout the first year, they will be engaged in an enormous contest of wills, each vying for power and leadership. And in the midst of this tug of war, she staggers out of the obstetrician's office with the words ringing in her ears, "I have some good news for you, Mrs. Jones!" If there is anything on earth Mrs. Jones doesn't need at that time, it is "good news" from an obstetrician.

From there to the final conflict, we see two disappointed, confused and deeply hurt young people, wondering how it all came about. We also see a little towheaded lad who will never enjoy the benefits of a stable home. He'll be raised by his mother and will always wonder, "Why doesn't Dad live here anymore?"

The picture I have painted does not reflect every young marriage, obviously, but it accurately represents far too many of them. The divorce rate is higher in America than in any other civilized nation in the world, and it is rising. In the case of our disillusioned young couple, what happened to their romantic dream? How did the relationship that began with such enthusiasm turn so quickly into hatred and hostility? They could not possibly have been more enamored with each other at the beginning, but their "happiness" blew up in their startled faces. Why didn't it last? How can others avoid the same unpleasant surprise?

First, we need to understand the true meaning of romantic love. Perhaps the answers to our quiz will help accomplish that objective.

1. *I believe love at first sight occurs between some people.*

Though some readers will disagree with me, love at first sight is a physical and emotional impossibility. Why? Because love is not simply a feeling of romantic excitement; it is more than a desire to marry a potential partner; it goes beyond intense sexual attraction; it exceeds the thrill at having "captured" a highly desirable social prize. These are emotions that are unleashed at first sight, but they *do not constitute love*. I wish the whole world knew that fact. These temporary feelings differ from love in that they place the spotlight on the one experiencing them. "What is happening to *me*?! This is the most fantastic thing *I've* ever been through! *I* think *I* am in love!" You see, these emotions are selfish in the sense that they are motivated by our gratification. They have little to do with the new lover. Such a person has not fallen in love with another person; *he has fallen in love with love*! And there is an enormous difference between the two.

The popular songs in the world of teen-age music reveal a vast ignorance of the meaning of love. One immortal number asserts, "Before the dance was throo, I knew I was in luv with yew." I wonder if the crooner will be quite so confident tomorrow morning. Another confesses, "I didn't know just what to do, so I whispered, 'I luv yew!'" That one really gets to me. The idea of basing a lifetime commitment on sheer confusion seems a bit shaky, at best. The Partridge Family recorded a song a few years ago which also betrays a lack of understanding of real love; it said, "I woke up in love today 'cause I went to sleep with you on my mind." You see, love in this sense is nothing more than a frame of mind— and it is just about that permanent. Finally, a rock group of the sixties called The Doors takes the prize for the most ignorant musical number of the century; it was called, "Hello, I Love You; Won't You Tell Me Your Name!"

Did you know that the idea of marriage based on romantic affection is a very recent development in human affairs? Prior to about 1200 A.D., weddings were arranged by the families of the bride and groom, and it never occurred to anyone that they were supposed to "fall in love." In fact, the concept of romantic love was actually popularized by William Shakespeare. There are times when I wish the old Englishman were here to help us straighten out the mess he initiated!

Real love, in contrast to popular notions, is an expression of the deepest appreciation for another human being; it is an intense awareness of his or her needs and longings—past, present, and future. It is unselfish and giving and caring. And believe me, friends, these are not attitudes one "falls" into at first sight, as though we were tumbling into a ditch. I have developed a lifelong love for my wife, but it was not something I fell into. I *grew* into it, and that process took time. I had to know her before I could appreciate the depth and stability of her character—to become acquainted with the nuances of her personality, which I now cherish. The familiarity from which love has blossomed simply could not be generated on "Some enchanted evening, across a crowded room." One cannot love an unknown object, regardless of how attractive or sexy or nubile it is!

2. *I believe it is easy to distinguish real love from infatuation.*

The answer is, again, false. That wild ride at the start of a romantic adventure bears all the earmarks of a lifetime trip. Just try to tell a starry-eyed sixteen-year-old dreamer that he is not really in love . . . that he's merely infatuated. He'll whip out his guitar and sing you a song. "Young luv, true luv, filled with real emo-shun. Young luv, true luv, filled with true devo-shun!" He knows what he feels, and he feels great. But he'd better enjoy the roller coaster ride while it lasts, because it has a predictable end point.

I must stress this fact with the greatest emphasis: The exhilaration of infatuation is *never* a permanent condition. Period! If you expect to live on the top of that mountain, year after year, you can forget it! As I discussed in the second chapter, emotions swing from high to low to high in cyclical rhythm, and since romantic excitement is an emotion, it too will certainly oscillate. Therefore, if the thrill of sexual encounter is identified as genuine love, then disillusionment and disappointment are already knocking at the door.

How many vulnerable young couples "fall in love" with love on the first date . . . and lock themselves in marriage before the natural swing of their emotions has even progressed through the first dip? They then wake up one morning without that neat feeling and conclude that love has died. In reality, it was never there in the first place. They were fooled by an emotional "high." I was trying to explain this up-and-down characteristic of our psychological nature to a group of 100 young married couples to whom I was speaking. During the discussion period, someone asked one young man in the group why he got married so young, and he replied, "'Cause I didn't know 'bout that wiggly line until it was too late!" Alas, 'tis true. That wiggly line has trapped more than one young romanticist.

The "wiggly line" is manipulated up and down by the circumstances of life. Even when a man and woman love each other deeply and genuinely, they will find themselves supercharged on one occasion and emotionally bland on another! *However, their love is not defined by the highs and lows, but is dependent on a commitment of their will!* I attempted to express this thought to my wife on an anniversary card, written approximately six years ago. It is reproduced below.

To My Darlin' Little Wife, Shirley, on the Occasion of Our Eighth Anniversary

I'm sure you remember the many, many occasions during our eight years of marriage when the tide of love and affection soared high above the crest . . . times when our feeling for each other was almost limitless. This kind of intense emotion can't be brought about voluntarily, but it often accompanies a time of particular happiness. We felt it when I was offered my first professional position. We felt it when the world's most precious child came home from the maternity ward of Huntington Hospital. We felt it when the University of Southern California chose to award a doctoral degree to me. But emotions are strange! We felt the same closeness when the opposite kind of event took place; when threat and potential disaster entered our lives. We felt an intense

closeness when a medical problem threatened to postpone our marriage plans. We felt it when you were
hospitalized last year. I felt it intensely when I knelt
over your unconscious form after a grinding automobile accident.

I'm trying to say this: both happiness and threat
bring that overwhelming appreciation and affection
for our beloved sweethearts. But the fact is, most of
life is made up of neither disaster nor unusual hilarity.
Rather, it is composed of the routine, calm, everyday
events in which we participate. And during these
times, I enjoy the quiet, serene love that actually
surpasses the effervescent display, in many ways. It
is not as exuberant, perhaps, but it runs deep and
solid. I find myself firmly in that kind of love on
this Eighth Anniversary. Today I feel the steady and
quiet affection that comes from a devoted heart. I
am committed to you and your happiness, more now
than I've ever been. I want to remain your "sweetheart."

When events throw us together emotionally, we will
enjoy the thrill and romantic excitement. But during
life's routine, like today, my love stands undiminished.
Happy Anniversary to my wonderful wife. Your Jim

The key phrase in my statement is, "I am committed
to you." You see, my love for Shirley is not blown back
and forth by the winds of change . . . by circumstances
and environmental influences. Even though my fickle
emotions jump from one extreme to another, my commitment remains solidly anchored in place. I have
chosen to love my wife, and that choice is sustained by an
uncompromising will. "In sickness and in health; for
richer or poorer; for better or worse; from this day forward. . . ." This essential commitment of the will is
sorely missing in so many modern marriages. I love you,
they seem to say, as long as I feel attracted to you . . .

or as long as someone else doesn't look better . . . or as long as it is to my advantage to continue the relationship. Sooner or later, this uncommitted love will certainly vaporize.

How, then, can real love be distinguished from temporary infatuation? If the feeling is unreliable, how can one assess the commitment of his will? There is only one answer to that question: It takes time. The best advice I can give a couple contemplating marriage (or any other important decision) is this: make *no* important, life-shaping decisions quickly or impulsively, and when in doubt, stall for time. That's not a bad suggestion for all of us to apply.

3. *I believe people who sincerely love each other will not fight and argue.*

I doubt if this third item actually requires an answer. Some marital conflict is as inevitable as the sunrise, even in loving marriages. There is a difference, however, between healthy and unhealthy combat, depending on the way the disagreement is handled. In an unstable marriage, the hostility is usually hurled directly at the partner: "You never do anything right; why did I ever marry you? You are incredibly dumb and you're getting more like your mother every day." These personal comments strike at the heart of one's self-worth and produce an internal upheaval. They often cause the wounded partner to respond in like manner, hurling back every unkind and hateful remark he can concoct, punctuated with tears and profanity. The avowed purpose of this kind of in-fighting is to hurt, and the words will never be forgotten, even though uttered in a moment of irrational anger. Obviously, such vicious combat is extremely damaging to a marital relationship. Healthy conflict, on the other hand, remains focused on the issue around which the disagreement began: "You are spending money faster than I can earn it!" "It upsets me when you don't tell me you'll be late for dinner." "I was embarrassed when you made me look foolish at the party last night." These areas of struggle, though admittedly emotional and tense, are much less damaging to the egos of the opposing forces. A healthy couple can work through them by compromise and negotiation with few imbedded barbs to pluck out the following morning.

The ability to fight *properly* may be the most important concept to be learned by newlyweds. Those who never comprehend the technique are usually left with two alternatives: (1) turn the anger and resentment inward in silence, where it will fester and accumulate through the years, or (2) blast away at the personhood of one's mate. The divorce courts are well represented by couples in both categories.

4. *I believe God selects one particular person for each of us to marry, and he will guide us together.*

A young man whom I was counseling once told me that he awoke in the middle of the night with the strong impression that God wanted him to marry a young lady whom he had only dated casually a few times. They were not even going together at that moment and hardly knew each other. The next morning he called her and relayed the message which God had supposedly sent him during the night. The girl figured she shouldn't argue with God, and she accepted the proposal. They have now been married for seven years and have struggled for survival since their wedding day!

Anyone who believes that God guarantees a successful marriage to every Christian is in for a shock. This is not to say that he is disinterested in the choice of a mate, or that he will not answer a specific request for guidance on this all-important decision. Certainly, his will should be sought in such a critical matter, and I consulted him repeatedly before proposing to my wife. However, I do not believe that God performs a routine match-making service for everyone who worships him. He has given us judgment, common sense, and discretionary powers, and he expects us to exercise these abilities in matters matrimonial. Those who believe otherwise are likely to enter marriage glibly, thinking, "God would have blocked this development if he didn't approve of it." To such confident people I can only say, "Lotsa luck."

5. *I believe if a man and woman genuinely love each other, then hardships and troubles will have little or no effect on their relationship.*

Another common misconception about the meaning of "true love" is that it inevitably stands like the rock of Gibraltar against the storms of life. Many people apparently believe that love is destined to conquer all; the Beatles endorsed this notion with their song, "All we need is love, love, love is all we need." Unfortunately, we need a bit more.

Much of my professional life is currently being invested in the Division of Child Development, Childrens Hospital of Los Angeles. We see numerous genetic and metabolic problems throughout the year, most of which involve mental retardation in our young patients. The emotional impact of such a diagnosis on the families involved is sometimes devastating; even in stable, loving marriages, the guilt and disappointment of having produced a "broken" child often drive a wedge of isolation between the distressed mother and father. In a similar manner, the fiber of love can be weakened by financial hardships, disease, business setbacks, or prolonged separation.

In short, we must conclude that love is vulnerable to pain and trauma, and often wobbles when assaulted by life.

6. *I believe it is better to marry the wrong person than to remain single and lonely throughout life.*

Again, the answer is false. Generally speaking, it is less painful to be searching for an end to loneliness than to be embroiled in the emotional combat of a sour marriage. Yet the threat of being an "old maid" (a term I detest) causes many girls to grab the first train that rambles down the marital track. And too often, it offers a one-way ticket to disaster.

7. *I believe it is not harmful to have sexual intercourse before marriage, if the couple has a meaningful relationship.*

This item represents *the* most dangerous of the popular misconceptions about romantic love, both for individuals and for our future as a nation. During the past fifteen years we have witnessed the tragic disintegration of our sexual mores and traditional concepts of morality. Responding to a steady onslaught by the entertainment industry and by the media, our people have begun to believe that premarital intercourse is a noble experience, and extramarital encounters are healthy, and homosexuality is acceptable, and bisexuality is even better. These views reflect the sexual stupidity of the age in which we live, yet they are believed and applied by millions of American citizens. A recent study of college students revealed that 25 percent of them have shared bedrooms with a member of the opposite sex for at least three months. According to *Life Styles and Campus Communities,* 66 percent of college students reportedly believe premarital intercourse is acceptable between any two people who consent or "when a couple has dated some and care a lot about each other." I have never considered myself to be a prophet of doom, but I am admittedly alarmed by statistical evidence of this nature. I view these trends with fear and trepidation, seeing in them the potential death of our society and our way of life.

Mankind has known intuitively for at least fifty centuries that indiscriminate sexual activity represented both an individual and a corporate threat to survival. The wisdom of those years has now been documented. Anthropologist J. D. Unwin conducted an exhaustive study of the eighty-eight civilizations which have existed in the history of the world. Each culture has reflected a similar life cycle, beginning with a strict code of sexual conduct and ending with the demand for complete "freedom" to express individual passion. Unwin reports that *every* society which extended sexual permissiveness to its people was soon to perish. There have been no exceptions.

Why do you suppose the reproductive urge within us is so relevant to cultural survival? It is because the energy which holds a people together is sexual in nature! The physical attraction between men and women causes them to establish a family and invest themselves in its development. It is this force which encourages them to work and save and toil to insure the survival of their families. This sexual energy provides the impetus for the raising of healthy children and for the transfer of values from one generation to the next. It urges a man to work when he would rather play. It causes a woman to save when she would rather spend. In short, the sexual aspect of our nature—when released exclusively within the family—produces stability and responsibility that would not otherwise occur. And when a nation is composed of millions of devoted, responsible family units, the entire society is stable and responsible and resilient.

If sexual energy within the family is the key to a healthy society, then its release outside those boundaries is potentially catastrophic. The very force which binds a people together then becomes the agent for its own destruction. Perhaps this point can be illustrated by an analogy between sexual energy in the nuclear family and physical energy in the nucleus of a tiny atom. Electrons, neutrons, and protons are held in delicate balance by an electrical force within each atom. But when that atom and its neighbors are split in nuclear fission (as in an atomic bomb), the energy which had provided the internal stability is then released with unbelievable power and destruction. There is ample reason to believe that this comparison between the atom and the family is more than incidental.

Who can deny that a society is seriously weakened when the intense sexual urge between men and women becomes an instrument for suspicion and intrigue within millions of individual families . . . when a woman never knows what her husband is doing when away from home . . . when a husband can't trust his wife in his absence . . . when half of the brides are pregnant at the altar . . . when each newlywed has slept with numerous partners, losing the exclusive wonder of the marital bed . . . when everyone is doing his own thing, particularly that which brings him immediate sensual gratification! Unfortunately, the most devastated victim of an immoral society of this nature is the vulnerable little child who hears his parents scream and argue; their tension and frustrations spill over into his world, and the instability of his home leaves its ugly scars on his young mind. Then he watches his parents separate in anger, and he says, "goodbye" to the father he needs and loves. Or perhaps we should speak of the thousands of babies born to unmarried teenage mothers each year, many of whom will never know the meaning of a warm, nurturing home. Or maybe we should discuss the rampant scourge of venereal disease which has reached epidemic proportions among America's youth. This is the true vomitus of the sexual revolution, and I am tired of hearing it romanticized and glorified. God has clearly forbidden irresponsible sexual behavior, not to deprive us of fun and pleasure, but to spare us the disastrous consequences of this festering way of life. Those individuals, and those nations, which choose to defy his commandments on this issue will pay a dear price for their folly. My views on this subject may be unpopular, but I believe them with everything within me!

8. *I believe if a couple is genuinely in love, that con-dition is permanent, lasting a lifetime.*

Love, even genuine love, is a fragile thing. It must be maintained and protected if it is to survive. Love can perish when a husband works seven days a week . . . when there is no time for romantic activity . . . when he and his wife forget how to talk to each other. The keen edge in a loving relationship may be dulled through the routine pressures of living, as I experienced during the early days of my marriage to Shirley. I was working full time and trying to finish my doctorate at the University of Southern California. My wife was teaching school and maintaining our small home. I remember clearly the eve-ning that I realized what this busy life was doing to our relationship. We still loved each other, but it had been too long since we had felt a spirit of warmth and close-ness. My text books were pushed aside that night and we went for a long walk together. The following semester I carried a very light load in school and postponed my academic goals so as to preserve that which I valued more highly.

Where does your marriage rank on your hierarchy of values? Does it get the leftovers and scraps from your busy schedule, or is it something of great worth to be pre-served and supported? It can die if left untended.

9. *I believe short courtships (six months or less) are best.*

The answer to this question is incorporated in the reply to the second item regarding infatuation. Short courtships require impulsive decisions about lifetime commitments, and that is risky business, at best.

10. *I believe teen-agers are more capable of genuine love than are older people.*

If this item were true, then we would be hard pressed to explain why half the teen-age marriages end in divorce in the first five years. To the contrary, the kind of love I have been describing—unselfish, giving, caring commitment—requires a sizeable dose of maturity to make it work. And maturity is a partial thing in most teen-agers. Adolescent romance is an exciting part of growing up, but it seldom meets the criteria for the deeper relationships of which successful marriages are composed.

Summary

All ten items on this brief questionnaire are false, for they represent the ten most common misconceptions about the meaning of romantic love. I wish the test could be used as a basis for issuing marriage licenses: those scoring 9 or 10 would qualify with honor; those getting 5-8 items right would be required to wait an extra six months before marriage; those dummies answering four or fewer items correctly would be recommended for permanent celibacy. To which group would you be assigned?

Questions and Answers

Question: I have often wondered why women seem to need romantic involvement so much more than men. Why do you think emotional coolness is a greater agitation to wives than to their husbands?

Answer: An unknown portion of this romantic need in women is probably related to genetic influences implemented by the hypothalamus region in the brain. Beyond this, the characteristic features probably result from differences in early experiences of girls and boys. The entire orientation for little girls in our society is toward romantic excitement. It begins during the preschool years with childhood fantasies, such as Cinderella dazzling the crowd (and particularly the Prince) with her irresistible charm, or Sleeping Beauty, being tenderly kissed back to consciousness by the handsome young man of her dreams. While little boys are identifying with football superstars and gun toting cowboys, their sisters are playing "Barbie

Dolls" and other role-oriented games which focus on dating and heterosexual relationships. Later, the typical high school girl will spend much more time daydreaming about marriage than will her masculine counterpart. He will think about sex, to be sure, but she will be glassy-eyed over love. She will buy and read the romantic pulp magazines . . . not he! Thus, males and females come to marriage with a lifelong difference in outlook and expectation.

Question: Why, then, are men so uninformed of this common aspect of feminine nature?

Answer: They haven't been told. For centuries, women have been admonished to meet their husbands' sexual needs—or else. Every female alive knows that the masculine appetite for sex demands gratification, one way or the other. What I have been attempting to say is that a woman's need for emotional fulfillment is just as pressing and urgent as the physiological requirement for sexual release in the male. Both can be stymied, but at an enormous cost! And as such, it is as unfortunate for a man to ignore his wife's need for romantic love as it is for her to foreclose on his sexual appetite.

For the benefit of my masculine readers, let me restate my message more directly: your wife is probably more vulnerable to your warmth and kindness than you have realized heretofore. Nothing builds her esteem more effectively than for you to let her (and others) know that you respect and value her as a person. And nothing destroys her self-confidence more quickly than your ridicule or rejection. If you doubt this fact, I urge you to conduct a simple experiment. At the breakfast table tomorrow morning, spontaneously tell your children how fortunate they are to have the mother whom God has given them. Without speaking directly to her, tell them how hard she works to keep them clean and well fed, and then mention how much you appreciate and love her. Just drop these words casually into the middle of your conversation while she is scrambling the eggs. Her reaction will give you valuable insight into her emotional state. If she goes into shock and burns the eggs, then it has definitely been too long since you gave her an unsolicited compliment. If she flashes a mischievous smile and suggests that you miss the 8:05 train this once, you'll then know how to cure the headaches she's been having at bedtime each evening. But if she fails to notice your comments, you must recognize that she is in critical condition and can only be resuscitated by taking her on a weekend trip to a nearby resort, at which time you will have flowers, candy and a love letter waiting in the selected motel.

How long has it been since you *consciously* attempted to convey respect to your wife?

Question: Do most women still want a strong husband who will assume leadership in their home?

Answer: Someone said, "A woman wants a man she can look up to, but one who won't look down on her." That quotation is very old, but it has weathered the Women's Liberation Movement and is still rather accurate. Again, a woman is usually comfortable in following masculine leadership if her man is loving, gentle, and worthy of her respect.

Question: I am a nineteen-year-old girl and I'm still single. You have described some pretty depressing circumstances that can occur in marriage. If that's the way it is, why should I bother to get married at all?

Answer: The depressing problems we've been examining represent the worst in married life; perhaps we have not spent enough time reviewing the more positive aspects. I can tell you from a personal point of view that my marriage to Shirley is the best thing that ever happened to me, and there are millions who can offer a similar testimony. You see, life involves problems no matter what your choices are; if you remain single, your frustrations will be of a different nature but they will occur, nevertheless. As to whether you should get married or not, I would offer you the same advice given me when I was an eight-year-old child, by a Sunday school teacher whose name I don't even remember: "Don't marry the person you think you can live with; marry the person you think you can't live without . . . if such an individual ever comes along." Either way, I think you're ahead by knowing in advance that married life offers no panacea —that if it is going to reach the potential, it will require an all-out investment by both husband and wife.

CHAPTER SIX

Financial Difficulties

When I was a teen-ager, I had a recurring dream which invariably delighted me: the episode would always begin by my noticing a shiny dime near the sidewalk where I walked. As I reached down to retrieve it, two quarters would be uncovered in the soil. By grabbing those two coins, at least four half-dollars would appear underneath, and it was obvious that I had stumbled onto a numismatic fortune. I would begin shoveling money by the handfuls, while looking over my shoulder. Always standing or walking nearby were dozens of people who hadn't noticed my discovery, and I was anxiously trying to stuff the cash in my pockets before being mobbed by competitors. There were slight variations to this theme (once I found millions of S&H Green Stamps,) but a distinct element of greed was always represented. Now, twenty years later, I'm happy to say that I've recovered from this greedy nature; instead, I frequently dream that I'm standing immobilized while everyone else finds the money! That's what twenty years of taxes and creditors have done to my adolescent aspirations.

What role do financial problems play in *your* mental life? It is likely that money matters are troubling to you too, because this item produces worry and anxiety for the entire human family. Financial stress certainly affected the women who completed our Sources of Depression questionnaire, for it ranked as their fifth most troubling difficulty. Remember also that this survey was obtained two years ago when inflation was less threatening than it is today; now it seems that every business, every school, every hospital and every home is struggling for financial survival. Furthermore, the hemorrhage of gold into the oil-producing nations of the Middle East may continue to plague the rest of the world—meaning the worst may be ahead. If economic depression comes, we may *all* have to learn to cope with its emotional consequence.

There are thousands of books available for those who want to gain control of their monetary resources, and I am no authority on that subject. Thus, my comments on this topic will be brief and to the point. My one contribution is in oppostion to the lust for more and more things— leading us to buy that which we neither need nor can afford.

Though I can make no claim to wealth, I have tasted most of the things Americans hunger for: new cars, an attractive home and gadgets and devices which promise to set us free. Looking at those materialistic possessions from the other side of the cash register, I can tell you that they don't deliver the satisfaction they advertise! On the contrary, I have found great wisdom in the adage, "That which you own will eventually own you!" How true that is. Having surrendered my hard earned dollars for a new object only obligates me to maintain and protect it; instead of its contributing to my pleasure, I must spend my precious Saturdays oiling it, mowing it, painting it, repairing it, cleaning it, or calling the Salvation Army to haul it off. The time I might have invested in worthwhile family activities is spent in slavery to a depreciating piece of junk.

Last summer I examined a swing set which was on display in a local toy store. It was shiny and well constructed, so I purchased an identical model for my children. When the delivery men arrived, however, they left me with a long box containing 6324 pipes, 28,-487,651 bolts, 28,487,650 screws, and a set of instructions that would make Albert Einstein swear and bite his nails. For the next forty-eight hours, I sweated to accommodate bent parts, missing parts, and parts from a 1948 Ford thrown in just to confuse me. Finally, the wobbly construction sat upright, though by this time I had mauled the knuckles on my right hand while trying to force a half-inch screw through a ⅜″ hole. However, the crusher came as I read the final line printed on the back side of the instructions; it said, "Please retighten all the bolts on this apparatus *every two weeks* to insure its safety and durability." What better example of materialistic slavery could there be? Along with everything else which I dare not forget, I now have to devote every other Saturday to this tin monster, or else it'll gobble up my children! That, friends and neighbors, is the price of ownership.

Let me ask you to recall *the* most worthless, unnecessary expenditure you have made in the last year. Perhaps it was an electric can opener which now sits in the garage, or a suit of clothes which will never be worn. Do you realize that this item was not purchased with your money; it was bought with your time which you traded for money. In effect, you swapped a certain proportion of your allotted days on earth for that piece of junk which now clutters your home. Furthermore, no power on earth could retrieve the time which you squandered on its purchase. It is gone forever. We are investing our lives in worthless materialism, both in the original expenditures and on subsequent upkeep and maintenance.

Do I sound a bit preachy in this discourse? Perhaps it is because I am condemning my own way of life. I am sick of the tyranny of things! But I'm also addressing the "have nots," those multitudes who are depressed because they own so little. How many women today are overcome with grief because they lack something which either wasn't invented or wasn't fashionable fifty years ago? How many families are discontent with their two-bedroom house, when it would have been considered entirely adequate in the 1800s? How many men will have heart attacks this year from striving to achieve an ever-increasing salary? How many families will court financial ruin just to keep up with the Joneses, and then find to their dismay that the Joneses have refinanced and are ahead again?

Let me conclude this discourse with one more thought. The utter folly of materialism was dramatically emphasized during my most recent trip to England. As I toured the museums and historical buildings, I was struck by what I called "empty castles." Standing there in the lonely fog were the edifices constructed by proud men who thought they owned them. But where are those men today? All are gone and most are forgotten. The hollow castles they left behind stand as monuments to the physical vulnerability and impermanence of the men who built them. Not one has survived to claim his possession. As Jesus said of the rich fool who was about to die and leave his wealth, "Then whose will those things be which thou hast provided?" (Luke 12:20)

May I say with the strongest conviction that I want to leave more than "empty castles" behind me when I die. At thirty-eight years of age, I realize how rapidly my life is passing before my eyes. Time is like a well-greased string which slides through my taut fingers. I've tried vainly to hold it or even slow its pace, but it only accelerates year by year. Just as surely as the past twenty years evaporated so quickly, the next three or four decades will soon be gone. So there is no better time than now for me (and you) to assess the values which are worthy of my time and effort. Having made that evaluation, I have concluded that the accumulation of wealth, even if I could achieve it, is an insufficient reason for living. When I reach the end of my days, a moment or two from now, I must look backward on something more meaningful than the pursuit of houses and land and machines and stocks and bonds. Nor is fame of any lasting benefit. I will consider my earthly existence to have been wasted unless I can recall a loving family, a consistent investment in the lives of people, and an earnest attempt to serve the God who made me. Nothing else makes much sense, and certainly nothing else is worthy of my agitation! How about you?

Question: I know many people who make their financial decisions on the basis of astrology. Even their business dealings are influenced by their horoscopes. Will you comment on the practice of astrology and whether there are any scientific facts to support it.

Answer: Of all the social developments occurring in recent years, none reveals our spiritual poverty more than the current devotion to astrology. I have been amazed to observe how uncritically this foolish belief has been accepted by television personalities, politicians, and millions of American young people. Even France's former President, Georges Pompidou, admitted in a press conference that he consulted his astrologer before making important speeches or state decisions.

How ridiculous to think that Adolf Hitler, Queen Elizabeth, Harry Truman, William Shakespeare, Bing Crosby, Willy Mays, Ho Chi Minh, Golda Meir and I should have everything in common because all of us were born under the sign of Taurus! How stupid to suppose that the success of our business ventures, our health, and even our sex lives are predetermined by the position of the stars and planets on the day of our births! Yet, there are more than

10,000 astrologers currently working in the United States, offering advice on everything from business deals to the compatibility of a man and his dog.

There is not a scrap of scientific evidence to support the validity of such illogical and atheistic notions. In fact, it was an all-knowing astrologist who advised Hitler to attack Russia—his biggest mistake! Nevertheless, millions of believers consult their horoscopes to obtain daily truth and wisdom.

I was recently introduced to a famous Hollywood actor while we sat waiting to appear on a television talk program. My wife was with me to observe the interview, and the actor commented on her attractiveness. He said, "I'll bet you are a Sagittarius, because most pretty girls are born under that sign." I was so appalled by the silliness of his statement that I felt obliged to challenge what he said. Trying not to insult his intelligence (which was difficult), I asked him if he had made any effort to prove his hypothesis. I pointed out how simple it would be, for example, to check the birth date of every girl entered in next year's Miss America or Miss Universe contest. I soon learned that the best way to end a conversation with an astrologist is to begin talking about scientific evidence.

In 1960, the world's astrologers announced that the worst combination of planetary influences in 25,000 years would occur that year. Seven of the nine planets were to appear in a line, which meant bad news for Mother Earth! Indian soothsayers were going crazy in sheer fright, and American sky-gazers were predicting everything from the drowning of California to the cataclysmic end of the world. But the fateful day came and went, of course, with no more disasters than on any other day. The astrologers had overlooked one fundamental fact: Man's destiny is not controlled by the planets. Both man and the heavenly bodies are under the indisputable authority of Almighty God!

When astrological advice is broadcast on radio or television stations, the announcers often repeat a "disclaimer," saying they are not attempting to foster a serious belief in astrology and are providing the horoscopes for fun and entertainment. How about it, then? Is astrology just an amusing pastime for our enjoyment? What about those millions of Americans who depend on the stars to provide direction and meaning each day? Isn't it better that they believe in this myth than to believe in nothing at all? Should we foster a tolerant attitude toward astrology, or should it be seen as an insidious philosophy to be opposed wherever possible?

A widely quoted psychiatrist recently professed that he urges his patients to depend on their astrologers, even though he admits that their predictions are scientifically worthless. I couldn't disagree more totally! Astrology is not only mythological nonsense, but it is dangerous to those who accept its tenets. One serious concern is that it offers a substitute for rational judgment and wisdom. A young man or woman, for example, may choose a marital partner on the basis of compatibility of their charts, without proper regard for the lifetime implications of their decision. Others postpone or disregard needed action because of the "do nothing" advice printed in their horoscopes. There is no way to estimate how many important decisions are based on the stars each day, undoubtedly having a profound impact on family, business, and even governmental affairs. How risky it is to determine one's destiny by the flip of a fickle coin. The naive believer exchanges his understanding of the facts, his common sense, his experience, and his better judgment for a "know all—tell all" pulp magazine of forecasts. He reminds me of a man confidently leaning against the wind while standing on top of a ten-story building. His body is seemingly held in check as he teeters precariously over the edge of the structure. But sooner or later, the gusts will slacken and the man will suddenly plunge downward in panic. Likewise, the astrological convert is leaning against an apparition which cannot possibly hold him securely in place. Sooner or later, when troubling and fearful circumstances beset him (as will come to everyone), he will reach frantically for something stable and firm to grasp. But he will find little support in the myth and superstition on which he has been leaning. Please believe me when I say I am personally and professionally acquainted with individuals who have taken that frightening plunge. Some fun! Some entertainment!

But now we must deal with another very important question: Why are so many highly educated and intelligent people willing to pledge allegiance to a belief that is baseless and unsupportable? There are, I feel, three answers to that question:

1. In recent years, a tremendous spiritual vacuum has occurred in the lives of many people who previously believed in God. Now that their God is dead, they are desperate for a substitute who can offer some measure of meaning and purpose to life.

Accordingly, someone has said, "Superstition is the worm that exudes from the grave of a dead faith." In other words, human beings *must* have something in which to believe, and in the absence of a meaningful faith in God, reliance is placed in superstitious nonsense.

2. Astrology is the only "religion" which imposes no obligation on its followers. One does not have to go to church for it, pay tithes to it, obey it, sing praises to it, be moral and honest for it, or sacrifice for it. And certainly, its followers need not carry a cross nor die in its cause.

All one must do is read and believe the words of its self-appointed priests in the daily newspaper. (Or perhaps pay $3.75 for a supersignificant, individualized horoscope, autographed personally by an IBM computer!)

3. It would be unwise to underestimate the real force behind the current astrological interest; it is clearly the tool of Satan himself. Whenever astrologists do predict events accurately, it is because of the demonic insights of God's greatest adversary.

This is not merely my opinion on the subject, which isn't very important. It is clearly the viewpoint of God himself, as expressed repeatedly in his Holy Word. The following two quotations from *The Living Bible* will serve to summarize his commandments to us regarding the practice of astrology and sorcery:

Hear the word of the Lord, O Israel: Don't act like the people who make horoscopes and try to read their fate and future in the stars! Don't be frightened by predictions such as theirs, for it is all a pack of lies (Jeremiah 10:1-3).

Call out the demon hordes you've worshiped all these years. Call on them to help you strike deep terror into many hearts again. You have advisors by the ton—your astrologers and star-gazers, who try to tell you what the future holds. But they are as useless as dried grass burning in the fire. They cannot even deliver themselves! You'll get no help from them at all. Theirs is no fire to sit beside to make you warm! And all your friends of childhood days shall slip away and disappear, unable to help (Isaiah 47:12-15).

CHAPTER SEVEN

Sexual Problems in Marriage

The sixth and seventh most common sources of depression in women ended in a tie, according to our questionnaire, and once again, the two items are closely related in other ways. They were, *Sexual Problems in Marriage,* and *Menstrual and Physiological Problems.* For the purpose of convenience, however, we will deal with sexual problems in this chapter and menstrual difficulties in the next.

Though depression associated with sexual frustration appeared to rank relatively low among the seventy-five women, there is ample evidence to indicate its importance and power. More than half of the group put it in the top five; and certainly, every experienced marriage counselor has observed the fear and tension commonly associated with bedroom activities. One of the reasons this item appeared to be of lesser significance is found in the limitations of a "rank order" questionnaire. Something *has* to be last, even though it may lie only a tiny distance from the first. In other words an "ordinal" scale of this nature measures only relative ranking, rather than distance between items. If you don't understand that explanation, forget it. There are more important matters to consider.

In keeping with the theme of this book, our focus in this chapter will be with the aspects of sex *which women most wish their husbands understood.* I wish I could devote an entire book to this topic, and perhaps someday I will. For now, however, we must concentrate on two important issues which I believe to be most troubling to women. They are as follows:

1. The Critical Difference Between Men and Women

An effort has been underway for the past few years to prove that men and women are identical, except for the ability to bear children. Radical feminists have vigorously (and foolishly) asserted that the only distinction between the sexes is culturally and environmentally produced. Nothing could be farther from the truth; males and females differ biochemically, anatomically, and emotionally. In truth, they are unique in every cell of their bodies, for men carry a different chromosomal pattern than women. There is also considerable evidence to indicate that the hypothalamic region, located just above the pituitary gland in the mid-brain, is "wired" very uniquely for each of the sexes. Thus, the hypothalamus (known as the seat of the emotions) provides women with a different psychological frame of reference than that of men. Further, female sexual desire tends to be somewhat cyclical, correlated with the menstrual calendar, whereas males are acyclical. These and other features account for the undeniable fact that masculine and feminine expressions of sexuality are far from identical. Failure to understand this uniqueness can produce a continual source of marital frustration and guilt. Two of the more consequential differences in sexual appetite are worthy of particular note.

First, men are primarily excited by *visual* stimulation.

They are turned on by feminine nudity or peek-a-boo glimpses of semi-nudity. (Phyllis Diller said she had the first peek-a-boo dress: men would "peek" at her, and then they would "boo"!) Women, by contrast, are much less visually oriented than men. Sure, they are interested in attractive masculine bodies, but the physiological mechanism of sex is not triggered typically by what they see; woman are stimulated primarily by the sense of touch. Thus, we encounter the first source of disagreement in the bedroom: he wants her to appear unclothed in a lighted room, and she wants him to caress her in the dark.

Second (and much more important), men are not very discriminating in regard to the person living within an exciting body. A man can walk down a street and be stimulated by a scantily clad female who shimmies past him, even though he knows nothing about her personality or values or mental capabilities. He is attracted by her body itself. Likewise, he can become almost as excited over a photograph of an unknown nude model as he can in a face-to-face encounter with someone he loves. In essence, the sheer biological power of sexual desire in a male is largely focused on the physical body of an attractive female. Hence, there is some validity to the complaint by women that they have been used as "sex objects" by men. This explains why female prostitutes outnumber males by a wide margin and why few women try to "rape" men. It explains why a roomful of toothless old men can get a large charge from watching a burlesque dancer "take it all off." It reflects the fact that masculine self-esteem is more motivated by a desire to "conquer" a woman than in becoming the object of her romantic love. These are not very flattering characteristics of male sexuality, but they are well documented in the professional literature. All of these factors stem from a basic difference in sexual appetites of males and females.

Women are much more discriminating in their sexual interests. They less commonly become excited by observing a good-looking charmer, or by the photograph of a hairy model; rather, their desire is usually focused on a *particular* individual whom they respect or admire. A woman is stimulated by the romantic aura which surrounds her man, and by his character and personality. She yields to the man who appeals to her emotionally as well as physically. Obviously, there are exceptions to these characteristic desires, but the fact remains: sex for men is a more physical thing; sex for women is a deeply emotional experience.

Now, so what? How can this sexual distinction interfere with a marital relationship where genuine love is evident? Simply this: unless a woman feels a certain closeness to her husband at a particular time—unless she believes he respects her as a person—she may be unable to enjoy a sexual encounter with him. A man can come home from work in a bad mood, spend the evening slaving over his desk or in his garage, watch the eleven o'clock news in silence, and finally hop into bed for a brief nighttime romp. The fact that he and his wife have had no tender moments in the entire evening does not inhibit his sexual desire significantly. He sees her on her way to bed in her clingy nightgown and that is enough to throw his switch. But his wife is not so easily moved. She waited for him all day, and when he came home and hardly even greeted her, she felt disappointment and rejection. His continuing coolness and self-preoccupation put a padlock on her desires; therefore, she may find it impossible to respond to him later in the evening. Let me go one step further: when a woman makes love in the absence of romantic closeness, she feels like a prostitute. Instead of participating in a mutually exciting interchange between lovers, she feels used. In a sense, her husband has exploited her body to gratify himself. Thus, she may either refuse to submit to his request, or else she will yield with reluctance and resentment. The inability to explain this frustration is, I believe, a continual source of agitation to women.

If I had the power to communicate only one message to every family in America, I would specify the importance of romantic love to every aspect of feminine existence. It provides the foundation for a woman's self-esteem, her joy in living, and her sexual responsiveness. Therefore, the vast number of men who are involved in bored, tired marriages—and find themselves locked out of the bedroom—should know where the trouble possibly lies. Real love can melt an iceberg.

2. The Variability in Desire

Men and women also differ significantly in their manifestations of sexual desire. Recent research seems to indicate that the intensity of pleasure and excitation at the time of orgasm in women and ejaculation in men is about the same for both sexes, although the pathway to that climax takes a different route. Most men can become excited more quickly than women. They may reach a point of finality before their mates get their minds off the evening meal and what the kids will wear tomorrow morning. It is a wise man who recognizes this feminine inertia, and brings his wife along at her own pace. But thousands of women will end this day in frustration because their impatient husbands will race through intercourse like they are going to a fire. And then when the moment of supreme pleasure is over, the men will be overcome with sleep and their wives will stare at the ceiling and listen to the sounds of the night. There's nothing thrilling about that.

It is also obvious that men hunger for sexual release more consistently than do women. One young lady told me of a water ski trip she and her husband took with another couple whom I'll call Harvey and Fran. Harvey had never been on water skis and he was grossly unco-ordinated. He tried desperately to get on his feet again and again, only to splash headlong into the lake each time. For three hours they worked to teach Harvey to ski, but he spent more time submarining behind the boat than he did skimming on the surface. Exhaustion began to show on his reddened face, as his wobbly legs dis-integrated ever more quickly beneath him. Fran rode si-lently in the back of the boat, watching her utterly fa-tigued husband blowing bubbles and gasping for air. Then she solemnly turned to her companion and shook her head saying, "Would you believe he'll still want it when we get home tonight?"

Many women stand in amazement at how regularly their husbands desire sexual intercourse. In this in-stance, there is a matter which *husbands wish their wives knew about men.* When sexual response is blocked, males experience an *accumulating* physiological pressure which demands release. Two seminal vesicles (small sacs containing semen) gradually fill to capacity; as maximum level is reached, hormonal influences sensitize the man to all sexual stimuli. Whereas a particular woman would be of little interest to him when he is satisfied, he may be eroticized just to be in her presence when he is in a state of deprivation. A wife may find it difficult to comprehend this accumulating aspect of her husband's sexual appetite, since her needs are typically less urgent and pressing. Thus, she should recognize that his de-sire is dictated by definite biochemical forces within his body, and if she loves him, she will seek to satisfy those needs as meaningfully and as regularly as possible. I'm not denying that women have definite sexual needs which seek gratification; rather, I am merely explaining that abstinence is usually more difficult for men to tol-erate.

Getting back to the variability in sexual appetites, not only do men and women differ, but enormous differences occur *between women*. Human nature is infinitely complex, and that complexity is expressed in a wide variety of sexual desires, particularly in the feminine gender. To put it graphically, female sexuality (and most other human characteristics) is probably "normally distributed." See the graph illustrated below:

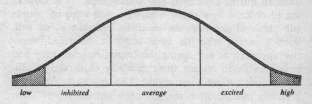

| low | inhibited | average | excited | high |

FEMALE SEXUAL DESIRE

The greatest number of women are represented by the center region of the curve, reflecting an "average" degree of sexual interest. The shaded area at the left reflects about two percent of the adult feminine population who have the least desire; they have been called frigid, cold, and unresponsive. The shaded area at the right symbolizes a comparable two percent at the maximum end of the distribution; this small group is composed of extremely sensual women who have been labeled "oversexed," nymphomaniacs, and less flattering descriptions. In between these divergent positions are ninety-six percent of the female population who are less extreme in sexual responses.

I have presented this diagram in order to discuss the often frustrated women who are represented by the lower half of this distribution. It is estimated that 20 to 25 percent of the adult females in our society exist in an "inhibited" zone, reflecting lukewarm or expressly negative attitudes toward sex. They rarely (if ever) experience orgasms and view intercourse as a marital duty and a chore to be endured. The bedroom holds no promise of the breathless thrills and chills so widely advertised. It is well worth our time to seek an understanding of these women, who often suffer constant mental anguish and anxiety.

First, why are some women less sensual than others?

Adult attitudes toward sexual relations are largely conditioned during childhood and adolescence. It is surprising to observe how many otherwise well-adjusted people still think of married sex as dirty, animalistic, or evil. Such a person who has been taught a one-sided, negative approach to sex during the formative years may find it impossible to release these carefully constructive inhibitions on the wedding night. The marriage ceremony is simply insufficient to reorient one's attitude from "Thou shalt not" to "Thou shalt—regularly and with great passion!" That mental turnabout is not easily achieved.

But I want to emphasize another factor: Not all differences in intensity of the sex drive can be traced to errors in childhood instruction. Human beings differ in practically every characteristic. Our feet come in different sizes; our teeth are shaped differently; some folks eat more than others, and some are taller than their peers. We are unequal creatures. Accordingly, we differ in sexual appetites. Our intellectual "computers" are clearly programed differently through the process of genetic inheritance. Some of us "hunger and thirst" after our sexuality, while others take it much more casually. My point is that we should learn to accept ourselves sexually, as well as physically and emotionally. This does not mean that we shouldn't try to improve the quality of our sex lives, but it does mean that we should stop struggling to achieve the impossible—trying to set off an atomic bomb with a matchstick! As long as a husband and wife are satisfied with each other, it doesn't matter what *Cosmopolitan* magazine says their inadequacies happen to be. Sex has become a statistical monster. "The average couple has intercourse three times a week! Oh No!

What's wrong with us? Are we undersexed?" A husband worries if his genitalia are of "average" size, while his wife contemplates her insufficient bust line. We are tyrannized by the great, new "sexual freedom" which has beset us. I hereby make a proposal: let's keep sex in its proper place; sure it is important, but it should serve us and not the other way around!

How does a sexually unresponsive woman feel?

It is certain that she is keenly aware of the erotic explosion which burns throughout her society. While her grandmother could have hidden her private inhibitions behind the protection of verbal taboo, today's woman is reminded of her inadequacy almost hourly. Radio, television, books, magazines, and movies make her think that the entire human race plunges into orgies of sexual ecstasy every night of the year. An inhibited wife can easily get the notion that the rest of America lives on Libido Lane in beautiful downtown Passion Park while she resides on the lonely side of Blizzard Boulevard. This unparalleled emphasis on genital gymnastics creates emotional pressure in enormous proportions. How frightening to feel sexless in a day of universal sensuality!

Sexual misfires—those icy bedroom encounters which leave both partners unsatisfied and frustrated—tend to be self-perpetuating. Unless each orgasm is accompanied by roman candles, skyrockets, and "The Stars and Stripes Forever," the fear of failure begins to gnaw on body and soul. Every disappointing experience is likely to interfere with the ability to relax and enjoy the next episode, which puts double stress on all those which follow. It is easy to see how this chain reaction of anxieties can assassinate whatever minimal desire was there in the first place. Then when sex finally loses its appeal, great emotions sweep down on the unresponsive lover. A woman who finds no pleasure in intercourse usually feels like a failure as a wife; she fears she may not be able to "hold" her husband who faces flirtatious alternatives at the office.

She experiences incredible guilt for her inability to respond, and inevitably her self-esteem gets clobbered in the process.

What does she do about her problems?

The distressing thing about sexual difficulties is that their treatment often seems worse than the disorder. Few of us relish the thought of revealing our most intimate and personal inadequacies to a person we neither know nor trust. To whom then does a woman turn for advice and counsel on such a delicate matter? A family physician or gynecologist may be consulted informally, but his training in the treatment of sexual dysfunctions is likely to be insufficient to resolve her problems. Furthermore, he lacks the time to provide the proper therapy. He may refer his patient to a psychiatrist, which is a pretty scary thought, in itself. If that suggestion is rejected or comes to naught, there are few alternatives. One does not ask one's next door neighbor for the name of a good sex therapist. In fact, the vast majority of America's sex therapy clinics are operated by frauds, charlatans, and outright quacks! One world-famous sex therapist asserts that fewer than 1 percent of the thousands of sex therapy clinics in the U.S. are legitimate. There is, then, no place for the inhibited woman to turn. She is blocked. Her problem has no solution. Her condition is without hope. No one seems to understand. Ultimately, the emotional pressure of that conflict often threatens to produce a physical blowout somewhere within.

I recently discussed the physical consequences of sexual inadequacy with Dr. David Hernandez, an obstetrician and gynecologist from the School of Medicine, University of Southern California, and the School of Medicine, Loma Linda University. He has observed an apparent increase in certain diseases and disorders since the advent of America's sexual revolution. It is Dr. Hernandez's opinion that his patients are under such pressure to perform in bed, and they experience such anxiety over their orgasmic inadequacies, that their physical health is adversely affected by the resulting stress. Emotional pressure usually makes itself known in certain psychosomatic "soft spots," including gastrointestinal (stomach) disorders, migraine headaches, high blood pressure, colonitis, and general fatigue. Dr. Hernandez believes, and I agree, that all of these medical problems are more prevalent among those who struggle to overcome sexual mediocrity.

Incidentally, Dr. Hernandez commented further that many men and women engage in sexual intercourse for reasons which God never intended. He listed a few of those illicit motives:

1. Sex is often permitted as a marital duty.
2. It is offered to repay or secure a favor.
3. It represents conquest or victory.
4. It stands as a substitute for verbal communication.
5. It is used to overcome feelings of inferiority (especially in men who seek proof of their masculinity).
6. It is an enticement for emotional love (especially by women who use their bodies to obtain masculine attention).
7. It is a defense against anxiety and tension.
8. It is provided or withheld in order to manipulate the partner.
9. It is engaged in for the purpose of bragging to others.

These "non-loving" reasons for participating in the sex act rob it of meaning and reduce it to an empty and frustrating social game. Sexual intercourse in marriage should bring pleasure, of course, but it should also provide a method of communicating a very deep spiritual commitment. Women are much more sensitive to this need.

How can husbands help?

The masculine member of the family can contribute

immeasurably to his wife's enjoyment—while enhancing his own—even in cases where her sexual appetite is on the weak side. Believe it or not, they can have a mutually rich and satisfying sex life if the husband understands how to bring it about. Here are the keys to feminine sensuality in situations where the physical drive is somewhat inhibited.

1. First, the romantic element is doubly or triply important as a prelude to intercourse in such cases. If a husband is too busy to be civil, then he should not expect his wife to exhibit any unusual desire or enjoyment in bed. She may satisfy his needs as an act of love and kindness, but her passion will not steam up their bedroom windows. For the woman represented by the "inhibited" zone on our normal distribution graph, a feeling of being loved and appreciated is usually the *only* route to excitation. This fact undoubtedly explains the remarkably high correlation on our questionnaire between *Sexual Problems* and *Lack of Romantic Love in Marriage*. Almost without exception, when one was rated near the top, the other was ranked similarly.

2. Secondly, a husband should recognize that some women do not have to experience orgasms in order to enjoy intercourse. Many wives can participate fully in sexual relations and feel satisfied at the conclusion even though there is no convulsing, ecstatic climax to the episode. (Other, more sensual women feel tremendous frustration if the tension and the vascular engorgement are not discharged.) The important thing is that the husband not *demand* that his wife experience orgasms, and he should certainly not insist that they occur simultaneously with his. To do this is to ask for the impossible, and it puts his wife in an unresolvable conflict. When the husband insists that his wife's orgasms be part of *his* enjoyment, she has but three choices: (1) She can lose interest in sex altogether, as happens with constant failure in *any* activity; (2) she can try and try and try

—and cry; or (3) she can "fake" it. Once a woman begins to bluff in bed, there is no place to stop. Forever after she must make her husband think she's on a prolonged pleasure trip, when in fact her car is still in the garage.

3. Perhaps the most dramatic contribution a husband can make to marital sexual relationships is to reverse the trend toward pressurized silence. When intercourse has been unenthusiastic, and when anxiety has been steadily accumulating, the tendency is to eliminate all reference to the topic in everyday conversation. Neither partner knows what to do about the problem, and they tacitly agree to ignore it. Even during sexual relations, they do not talk to one another. Though it seems impossible, an inhibited husband and wife can make love several times a week for a period of years without ever verbalizing their feelings or frustrations on this important aspect of their lives. When this happens, the effect is like taking a hot coke bottle and shaking it until the contents are ready to explode. Remember this psychological law: any anxiety-producing thought or condition which cannot be expressed is almost certain to generate inner pressure and stress. The more unspeakable the subject, the greater the pressurization. And as described in the previous section, anxious silence leads to the destruction of sexual desire.

Furthermore, when conversation is prohibited on the subject of sex, the act of intercourse takes on the atmosphere of a "performance"—each partner feeling that he is being critically evaluated by the other. To remove these communicative barriers, the husband should take the lead in releasing the safety valve for his wife. That is done by getting her to verablize her feelings, her fears, her aspirations. They should talk about the manners and techniques which stimulate—and those which don't. They should face their problems as mature adults . . . calmly and confidently. There is something magical to be found in such soothing conversation; tensions and anxieties are reduced when they find verbal expression. To the men of the world, I can only say, "Try it."

4. The fourth way husbands can increase the sensuality of their less passionate wives is by paying attention to the geography and techniques of intercourse. Women are more easily distracted than men; they are more affected by the surroundings and noises and smells than are their husbands. The possibility of being heard by the kids bothers women more, and they are more dependent on variety in manner and circumstances. Another rather common inhibitor to women, according to the concerns verbalized in counseling sessions, is the lack of cleanliness by their husbands. A service station operator or a construction worker may become sexually aroused by something he has seen or read during the day, causing him to desire intercourse with his wife as soon as he arrives home from his job. He may be sweaty and grimy from the day's work, smelling of body odor and needing to use some Crest on his teeth. Not only are his fingernails dirty, but his rough, calloused hands are irritating to his wife's delicate skin. An interference such as this can paralyze a woman sexually, and make her husband feel rejected and angry.

Spontaneity has its place in the marital bed, but "sudden sex" often results in "sudden failure" for a less passionate woman. In general, I believe sex should be planned for and prepared for and anticipated. For the man who has been dissatisfied with his recent sex life, I suggest that he call a local hotel or motel and make reservations for a given night, but tell no one about his plans. He should arrange secretly for the children to be cared for until morning, and then ask his wife to go out to dinner with him. After they have eaten a good meal, he should drive to the hotel without going home or announcing his intentions. The element of surprise and excitement should be preserved to the very last moment. Once inside the hotel room (where flowers may be waiting), the happy hormones will dictate the remainder of the instructions. My point is that sexual excitation requires a little creativity, particularly in cases of a "tired" relationship. For example, the widespread notion that males are inherently active and females are inherently passive in a sexual sense is nonsense; the freedom to express passion spontaneously is vital to enjoyment. When one makes love in the same old bedroom, from the same position and surrounded by the same four walls, it *has* to become rather routine after so many years. And routine sex is usually bored sex.

A physician named Schwab (who has undoubtedly heard every possible joke about his name) described the difficulties a woman may experience in playing the three unique roles expected of her; she must be a wife, mistress, and mother. A loving wife who is diligently maintaining her home and caring for the needs of her family is unlikely to feel like a seductive mistress who tempts her husband into the bedroom. Likewise, the requirements of motherhood are at times incompatible with the alternate roles of wife and mistress. Though these "assignments" seem contradictory, a woman is often asked to switch from one to another on short notice. Her husband can help by getting her away from the wife and mother responsibilities when it is time for her to be his mistress.

Someone said, "By the time I tuck the kids in, put the cat out, and take the telephone receiver off . . . who cares?!" It's a very valid question.

5. Another sexual "inhibitor" which husbands should understand is fatigue itself. Physical exhaustion plays a significant part in some women's ability (or inability) to respond sexually. By the time a mother has struggled through an eighteen-hour day—especially if she has been chasing an ambitious toddler or two—her internal pilot light may have flickered and gone out. When she finally

falls into bed, sex represents an obligation rather than a pleasure. It is the last item on her "to do" list for that day. Meaningful sexual relations utilize great quantities of body energy and are seriously hampered when those resources have already been expended. Nevertheless, intercourse is usually scheduled as the final event in an evening.

If sex is important in a marriage, and we all know that it is, then some time should be reserved for its expression. The day's working activities should end early in the evening, permitting a husband and wife to retire before exhausting themselves on endless chores and responsibilities. Remember this: *whatever* is put at the bottom of your priority list will probably be done inadequately. For too many families, sex languishes in last place.

Many of you have read Dr. David Reuben's best selling book entitled, *What You've Always Wanted to Know about Sex but Were Afraid to Ask.* (I bought Dr. Reuben's book because I've always liked his sandwich so well.) But after considering the frequent inhibitions caused by utter exhaustion, I think Dr. Reuben should have called his book, *What You've Always Wanted to Know about Sex but Were Too Tired to Ask!*

6. Finally, we should spend a moment or two discussing the relationship between self-esteem and sexual enjoyment. I said in the beginning of this book that every item on the Sources of Depression list is related to every other issue. That fact is certainly evident in the connection between self-worth and the ability to respond to sexual stimuli. A woman who feels ugly, for example, is often too ashamed of her imperfect body to participate in sex without embarrassment. She knows it is impossible to disguise forty-year-old thighs, and her flaws interfere with her sensuality. Sex for human beings is inseparably connected with our psychological nature. Hence, the person who feels shy and timid and inferior will usually express his sexuality in similar terms, or on

the other hand, the self-confident, emotionally healthy individual is more likely to have a fulfilling sex life. Therefore, a husband should recognize that anything which reduces his wife's self-esteem will probably be translated into bedroom problems. His ridicule of her small breasts or varicose veins or large buttocks, even in fun, may make her self-conscious and uncomfortable during future sexual encounters. Any disrespect which he reveals for her as a person is almost certain to crop up in their physical relationship, as well. In this regard, our sexual behavior differs radically from the mechanistic responses of lower animals. The emotional concomitants simply cannot be denied or suppressed in human beings.

There is so much more that could (and should) be said about the sexual relationship between men and women, although we must accede to space and time limitations. Perhaps the question and answer section which follows will permit the introduction of a few other important topics for consideration.

Questions and Answers

Question: Would you say that *most* marital problems are caused by sexual difficulties?

Answer: No, the opposite is more accurate. Most sexual problems are caused by marital difficulties. Or stated another way, marital conflicts occurring *in bed* are usually caused by marital conflicts occurring *out of bed*.

Question: Is it inevitable that sexual desire must diminish in the fifth, sixth, and seventh decades of life?

Answer: There is no organic basis for women or men to experience less desire as they age. The sexual appetite depends more on a state of mind and emotional attitudes than on one's chronological age. If a woman sees herself as old and unattractive, she might lose interest in sex for reasons only secondary to her age. But from a physical point of view, it is a myth that menopausal men and women must be sexually apathetic.

Question: It is my understanding that some women fail to enjoy sex because of weakness of the muscular structure in the pelvic region. Is this true? What can be done about it?

Answer: The late Dr. Arnold Kegel, professor of Obstetrics and Gynecology at USC School of Medicine, accumulated considerable evidence to show that sexual response is inhibited in women whose pubococcygeal muscle was flaccid. He offered simple exercises to tone up the muscle, and reported remarkable results for women who had previously been inorgasmic. There are other causes for sexual dysfunction, obviously, but for women who are interested in learning more about this physical explanation, I suggest they read *The Act of Marriage* by Tim LaHaye (Zondervan).

Question: Since masculine and feminine sexual appetites differ, do men and women usually enter an extramarital affair for different reasons?

Answer: Yes, men are more interested in the excitation of sexual intercourse, and women are more motivated by emotional involvement. This is why a woman often gets hurt in such an encounter, because the man loses interest in their relationship when his mistress ceases to stimulate him as before. Someone wrote, "Men love women in proportion to their strangeness to them." Although the word "love" is used inappropriately in that proverb, there is a grain of truth in its message.

Question: You stated that men and women are vastly different, not only with regard to cultural influences, but physiologically as well. Would you discuss these differences and their implications further?

Answer: Dr. Paul Popenoe, founder of the American Institute of Family Relations in Los Angeles, has written a brief article on the subject you have raised. I will let him respond to the question, *Are Women Really Different?*

"One of the least acceptable parts of the Women's Lib and related movements is the attempt to minify the differences between the sexes. The main thrust of their debate, or more correctly their assertions, is that such differences as exist are merely the result of differences in education and training, and therefore not basic. Since many of these differences, even if associated with education and training, have been maintained for a million years or more, it would indeed be surprising if they are not by this time deeply ingrained. But in fact, the sexes differ so markedly in ways that are not subject to change—anatomy and physiology—that it is a serious mistake to ignore them or to try to make them disappear by talking.

"Take a conspicuous difference, which is certainly not produced by education or training—the feminine function of menstruation. David Levy found that the depth and intensity of a woman's maternal instinct, her motherly feeling, is associated with the duration of her menstrual period and the amount of the flow. The extensive changes in the activity of her glands of internal secretion also produce marked differences in her behavior. In any large group of women of child-bearing age, 18% will be menstruating at any one time. Against this percentage, autopsies of women suicides find that 40%, 50%, even 60% were menstruating at the time they took their own lives.

"Dr. Katherina Dalton, in *The Premenstrual Syndrome* (Springfield, Ill., 1964) summarizes many studies of behavior change that show a large portion of women's crimes (63% in an English study, 84% in a French) are not distributed evenly over time, but clustered in the premenstrual period along with suicides, accidents, a decline in the quality of school work, decline in intelligence test scores, visual acuity, and response speed. In the United States, she calculated that absenteeism related to menstruation costs about five billion dollars a year, but accidents, absenteeism, and domestic quarrels are only part of the social repercussions of symptoms that affect everyone. "A book might be filled with discussion of other biological differences between the sexes, that are of great importance in one way or another, in everyday life, and are certainly not the outcome of differences in education, training, and social attitudes toward the two sexes. Here is a quick rundown of a few:

1. Men and women differ in every cell of their bodies. This difference in the chromosome combination is the basic cause of development into maleness or femaleness as the case may be.

2. Woman has greater constitutional vitality, perhaps because of this chromosome difference. Normally, she outlives man by three or four years, in the U.S.

3. The sexes differ in their basal metabolism— that of woman being normally lower than that of man.

4. They differ in skeletal structure, woman having a shorter head, broader face, chin less protruding, shorter legs, and longer trunk. The first finger of a woman's hand is usually longer than the third; with men the reverse is true. Boys' teeth last longer than do those of girls.

5. Woman has a larger stomach, kidneys, liver, and appendix, smaller lungs.

6. In functions, woman has several very important ones totally lacking in man—menstruation, pregnancy, lactation. All of these influence behavior and feelings. She has more different hormones than does man. The same gland behaves differently in the two sexes— thus woman's thyroid is larger and more active; it enlarges during pregnancy but also during menstruation; it makes her more prone to goiter, provides resistance to cold, is associated with the smooth skin, relatively hairless body, and thin layer of subcutaneous fat which are important elements in the concept of

personal beauty. It also contributes to emotional instability—she laughs and cries more easily.

7. Woman's blood contains more water (20% fewer red cells). Since these supply oxygen to the body cells, she tires more easily, is more prone to faint. Her constitutional viability is therefore strictly a long-range matter. When the working day in British factories, under wartime conditions, was increased from 10 to 12 hours, accidents of women increased 150%, of men not at all.

8. In brute strength, men are 50% above women.

9. Woman's heart beats more rapidly (80, vs. 72 for men); blood pressure (10 points lower than man) varies from minute to minute; but she has much less tendency to high blood pressure—at least until after the menopause.

10. Her vital capacity or breathing power is lower in the 7:10 ratio.

11. She stands high temperature better than does man; metabolism slows down less.'"

Question: Tell me why I shouldn't be totally free to do anything I want, as long as my behavior doesn't affect anyone else.

Answer: *Nothing* that you do is without influence on others. To illustrate this fact, let me ask you to take in a deep breath of air and hold it for a moment. The air that you inhaled contains at least three nitrogen atoms which were breathed by *every* human being who ever lived; literally, a portion of that same volume of air was inhaled by Jesus Christ, Abraham Lincoln, Leonardo da Vinci, and Spiro T. Agnew. In fact, your breath also contained at least three nitrogen atoms which were breathed by each of the dinosaurs of ancient times. Every living thing interacts with every other creature on earth, and the smallest act can reverberate for centuries.

Let me illustrate this interaction further. Suppose in

the year 1500, a seemingly insignificant event served to delay sexual intercourse in a couple who produced a child. By delaying conception, even by five minutes, it is likely that a different sperm cell would have penetrated the egg in the mother. That would mean that a different person would have been born as a result of that minute interference. There is a 50-50 chance that the sex would not even have been the same. Then, the influences of the person who might have been would be replaced by the impact of the person who was actually conceived, multiplied day by day throughout his lifetime. How many other conceptions would the replacement alter in a sixty-year period? It is impossible to measure, but the impact of that original act would echo through the decades, perhaps resulting in a totally *different* population on earth than exists today. Just imagine, for example, how different the world would be today if Adolf Hitler's sibling had been conceived instead of the tyrannical dictator.

In short, it is incredibly foolish to think we can do *anything* without affecting our associates and fellow citizens on this earth. For this reason I react with irritation to the idiotic motto of the dropout culture, "If it feels good—do it."

Question: I am becoming increasingly discouraged by the television programs coming into my home. Will you comment on the impact of the TV industry on our society?

Answer: Television has an enormous capacity to influence every aspect of our lives, from our attitudes toward politicians down to the nitty-gritty of everyday living. Did you know that the big tube even determines when we visit the bathroom? I'm told that workmen employed in large city sewers can tell precisely when the commercials occur on major programs because the viewers all flush their toilets at once. That has to be the most earthy example of television's power to govern our behavior.

The effectiveness of this medium makes its corruption all the more dangerous. Television's current obsession with cops and robbers and homosexuals and prostitutes and violence and rape and illicit sex are certain to perpetuate the real thing in everyday life. I have been most distressed with the consistent attack on traditional family life, which is ridiculed and criticized every night of the year. The Merv Griffin Show, for example, often seems singularly devoted to the destruction of marriage as an institution. My disgust at this constant vilification led me to write the following personal letter to Mr. Griffin on December 17, 1974.

Mr. Merv Griffin
Griffin Productions
1735 Vine Street
Hollywood, California 90028

Dear Mr. Griffin:

Having watched your television show intermittently for the past four years, I can no longer remain silent about a matter which causes me great concern and agitation. Night after night, your program has clearly been dedicated to the destruction and dismemberment of the traditional American family. You and your guests have presented an incessant bombardment on the institution of marriage, sexual fidelity, dedication to parenthood, and every other essential component of successful family living. Most importantly, you have seldom permitted a balancing viewpoint from those who represent the opposite thesis.

My point is best illustrated by the comments made on a typical show, aired in Los Angeles on Monday, December 9, 1974. That program featured two hours of nonstop venom, some of which is quoted (or paraphrased) below:

John Byner, your first guest, explained that he had been divorced for nine years, and was raising his two girls alone. He said it was a highly successful arrangement.

Pamela Mason then blasted onto the screen, saying she was strongly opposed to the concept of marriage. "It's just a two-dollar piece of paper from a rotten government which tries to tell us who we can sleep with." She also said she was married to James Mason for thirty years and cheated on him at least fifty times during that period. She said she wouldn't recognize his voice if he called her on the phone today. Mrs. Mason concluded her remarks by saying the problem in the world today is that we have too much religious fervor. "We need to get rid of that!" she asserted.

Chip (last name missed) then joined you on camera, and sang a song about the impermanence of man-woman relationships, entitled "All Is Fair in Love."

Carole Cook was then invited on the set. When the subject of sexual loyalty was introduced, she said, "I'm as pure as the driven slush." You and Mrs. Mason teased her about being married to a previously divorced man, asserting scornfully that she was "living in sin." Mrs. Cook replied, "Oh! I just love that." (audience laughter) She explained that she wasn't keen on marriage because it requires people to "talk to their mate about their actions and behavior."

Rubin Carson was then invited to join the group. He began his contribution by saying he was "working on a movie on the subject of Open Marriage, studying the effects of not being faithful in a marriage." He said he had been married three times and favored divorce to infidelity. He claimed to have just finished writing a book entitled, *Sex Is Nature's Way of Saying, Hi!*

Thus, two more hours of destructive propaganda were injected directly into the veins of the American home, where it could rot us from within. At least the Trojan Horse contained soldiers who were recognized as the enemy; you have invaded us with insidious philosophies, carefully disguised as humor and entertainment. How many teen-agers and children watched your show on December 9, each comparing his values to the foolish advice regurgitated by your guests? (They'll hear it again tomorrow night, and again and again and again.) How many wives found in your words the courage they needed to abandon their responsibilities at home? How many husbands decided during your program to accept those extramarital sexual opportunities they had been declining? How many children will someday have you to blame for the disintegration of everything stable in their lives? I can't supply the numerical answers to these questions, but I do know you and your colleagues are systematically undermining the foundation of the family. And when it collapses, you and I and the rest of our society will disintegrate with it.

I have only one voice, but I am going to do my best to make it heard on this subject. I hope, at the very least, to bring pressure upon you to allow another viewpoint to be represented in your future programming.

Most sincerely,
James C. Dobson, Ph.D.
Assistant Professor of Pediatrics
USC School of Medicine

Copies of this statement were sent to the Federal Communication Commission and to Mr. John Kluge, president of Metromedia, Inc. Neither Mr. Griffin nor Mr. Kluge even bothered to reply to my letter. The FCC sent me a printed explanation saying they could not interfere with the expression of free speech. And the beat goes on.

This "untouchable" characteristic of television makes it devastatingly effective in influencing the mores and values of our society. Never in the history of mankind has there been a comparable force with such power to rewrite social customs and values in so brief a time. Once an objective has been agreed upon, the populace is bombarded night and day with that incessant theme, fitting it into every drama, every news program, and every afternoon soap opera. The current campaign is devoted to reconstructing the role of women in America. One simple message is dramatized in a thousand creative ways: If you are at home raising children, you are being cheated, bored, exploited, and wasted as a human being. Why don't you put some meaning in your life and get into the business world with the rest of your sisters? To sell this idea more effectively, women are cast as policewomen, surgeons, newspaper editors, or *anything* other than wives and mothers.

While there is nothing wrong with a woman choosing to be a surgeon or newspaper editor, I resent the underlying message that motherhood and housework are affronts to feminine dignity. It is also irritating to see the duplicity of the producers who offer their programs as entertainment, when their real motive is to change the structure of the American home.

How does one oppose such a powerful force when it is unresponsive to the majority? We badly need an answer to that question. The bias of the media was illustrated to me last month when I sat by a woman physician on a plane from Phoenix to Los Angeles. She was working for the Right to Life Association which is opposed to the continuation of indiscriminant abortions. (900,000 *known* abortions took place in America in 1974.) She expressed great agitation over the censure of the anti-abortion viewpoint in newspapers, magazines, and on television. Earlier this year, 50,000 women marched on

Washington, D.C., carrying signs and distributing literature on behalf of Right to Life legislation. *Newsweek* and *Time* magazines each sent reporters to cover the event, as did the wire services and television networks. *Not a single one* of these communicative sources actually reported the event. The leaders were told that the march was not newsworthy! The following week, however, fewer than twenty representatives of the proabortion forces also marched on Washington, and their words and actions were broadcast across the nation that evening. In this case, 50,000 were ignored and twenty were given total coverage. The physician said that this typifies the impossible barrier to publicity which her organization has consistently experienced.

I would like to propose a solution to the bias that we face by the media. While I have neither the time nor the resources to implement this suggestion, perhaps someone among my readers will be able to apply it. What we desperately need is a central office which would receive and register our complaints en masse. Instead of writing the station, as I did ineffectively with Mr. Griffin, our message of objection would be sent to a coordinating staff which would then transmit our views to the executives who have ignored our individual voices. The name of the game is numbers. If this central office could tell the network that 100,000 letters were on file in opposition to a particular program, the voltage would be a million times greater than from a relatively few objections scattered in different places. Even more effectively, the sponsors of an offensive program could be told that their product would be boycotted if they continued to support such material. On the other hand, the coordinating service could also reinforce constructive programming, offering appreciation and praise where it is warranted. This valuable service could be underwritten for perhaps $5 per year from those who are now unrepresented by the media, and might even be supported by church denominations and other organizations that believe in the family and want to preserve it. If we do not have such methods of relaying our collective views, television executives have the power to hammer their ideas into our homes throughout the year, and we are impotent to influence them.

Question: In keeping with your comments about the role of women, it seems to me that a reverse discrimination is now being shown, with women being characterized as vastly superior to men. Do you agree?

Answer: The image of women now being depicted by the media is a ridiculous combination of wide-eyed fantasy and feminist propagada. Today's woman is always shown as gorgeous, of course, but she is more—much more. She roars around the countryside in a racy sports car, while her male companion sits on the other side of the front seat anxiously biting his nails. She exudes self-confidence from the very tips of her fingers, and for good reason: she could dismantle any man alive with her karate chops and flying kicks to the teeth. She is deadly accurate with a pistol and she plays tennis (or football) like a pro. She speaks in perfectly organized sentences, as though her spontaneous remarks were being planned and written by a team of tiny English professors sitting in the back of her pretty head. She is a sexual gourmet, to be sure, but she wouldn't be caught dead in a wedding ceremony. She has the grand good fortune of being perpetually young, and she never becomes ill, nor does she ever make a mistake or appear foolish. In short, she is virtually omniscient, except for a curious inability to do anything traditionally feminine, such as cook, sew, or raise children. Truly, today's screen heroine is a remarkable specimen, standing proud and uncompromising, with wide stance and hands on her hips. Oh, yeah! This baby has come a *long, long* way, no doubt about that.

I suppose I object to this phony image of women because of the hypocrisy represented by those who have created it. Our confident superchick is the product of a movement which despises the same ridiculous fantasy in the masculine world. So much has been said about the follies of the male ego—of the intolerable pride and haughtiness in mankind the world over. In fact, most of the woes faced by women today have been blamed on self-appointed supermen who feed their self-esteem at the expense of females. But if masculine egotism is an evil (and it is), then why are its opponents working so hard to create a feminine version of the same defect? These contradictory campaigns are waged with equal vigor, condemning male supremacy with one breath and propagating female superiority with the next. Why don't we admit that haughty pride is disgusting wherever it is found, and superwomen are every bit as rare as fast-living, karate-chopping, bullet-proof members of the male population.

Question: What is bisexuality and why are we hearing so much about it now?

Answer: A bisexual is someone who participates in both heterosexual and homosexual acts of passion. At the time of this writing, bisexuality is the fad among swingers and is getting enormous amounts of publicity in the American press. The cover of a recent *Cosmopolitan* magazine posed the question, "Is Bisexuality Thinkable (or Even Do-able) for Non-nut Cases?" Inside, the caption read, "Could *you* be ready for a lesbian encounter? Well, a surprising number of perfectly 'normal' man-loving females are——." The article concluded with this statement: "Whether or not we're all predestined to be bisexual remains in question. Still, whatever happens in the future, I've concluded that, right now, for the many who've tried it, bisexuality offers a satisfying—and often loving—way of life."[2]

Vogue magazine carried a similar feature story with the same message. Alex Comfort, writing in *More Joy*, predicted that bisexuality will be the standard, middle-class morality within ten years. And on a recent television program aired in Los Angeles on Saturday morning—a time when the greatest numbers of children are watching —four aggressive lesbians were featured. They were not just discussing their sexual preferences; they were advocating female homosexuality with all the militant enthusiasm they could generate. A viewer recorded the discussion and sent me a word-for-word transcript of the program, which included this summary statement by one of the participants: "Someone asked me if I was afraid my children would become lesbians. And I said, 'I should be so lucky.' " (Incidentally, guess who has turned up as the moderator of the program described above; it is the militant feminist who appeared as the "other guest" on the television program mentioned on page thirty-three of this book. You see, her anger *did* pay off.)

Is it any wonder that homosexuality is considered "contagious"? It spreads, and this kind of publicity is the vehicle for its propagation. Sometimes I think we have become so blind to evil that we wouldn't recognize immorality if it were an elephant coming through the door. Someone would say, "It's just a mouse with a glandular condition," and everyone would nod in agreement.

I'm reminded of the eternal words of the prophet Isaiah, writing in the Old Testament: "Woe unto them that call evil good and good evil; that put darkness for light, and light for darkness; that put bitter for sweet, and sweet for bitter . . . Therefore, as the fire devoureth the stubble, and as the flame consumeth the chaff, so their root shall be as rottenness and their blossom shall go up as dust: because they have cast away the law of the Lord of hosts, and despised the word of the Holy One of Israel" (5:20, 24).

Morality and immorality are not defined by man's changing attitudes and social customs. They are determined by the God of the universe, whose timeless standards cannot be ignored with impunity!

CHAPTER EIGHT

Menstrual and Physiological Problems

In October 1959, my mother suddenly began to deteriorate physically and emotionally. She became extremely nervous and irritable, and experienced unrelenting depression for weeks at a time. Her face was drawn and the area around her eyes was black and hollow. She made an appointment with a physician who examined her and diagnosed her symptoms as emotional in origin. He prescribed a tranquilizer to "calm her nerves," although the medication had precisely the opposite effect. It made her feel like climbing the walls. She visited a second doctor who made the same diagnosis and prescribed a different tranquilizer. It had the same consequence. She continued to search for an answer to the distressing disorder which had beset her, but no one seemed to know what to do. Six physicians were consulted, each diagnosing her problem as being psychological in nature, prescribing medications which only aggravated her difficulties further.

My mother began to lose weight and she found it more difficult to cope with the responsibilities of everyday living. She became preoccupied with her own death, and on one occasion called me on the telephone to tell me the clothes in which she wished to be buried. My father and I knew this was not characteristic of her, and we agreed that she was deteriorating rapidly. The next day I called a physician who had been a friend of our family for several decades. "Paul," I said with concern, "you are going to have to help me with my mother, because we are rapidly losing her." He asked me to describe her symptoms, which I did. He listened to the details for a few moments and then interrupted to say, "Send your mother to see me. I can help her."

The next morning, my mother went to see the physician with whom I had consulted. He determined that she was in a state of extreme estrogen deprival as a consequence of menopause, and he prescribed an immediate injection of this essential hormone. She returned a week later for a second injection, and continued every seven days for years to come. Though her "cure" did not occur instantaneously, the effect of the medication was like turning from darkness to light. Her depression vanished; her dark eyes returned to normal; she became interested in life again and the woman we had known and loved through the years was with us once more.

My mother's emotional and physical health remained stable for ten years, until she and my father moved 1500 miles away from the physician who had provided the essential estrogen. Once again, the search for an understanding doctor began. The man to whom she turned said he disagreed with the diagnosis, but he would prescribe estrogen simply because she seemed to be doing so well at that time. "Why change a winning combination?" he commented. However, one day when she arrived for her weekly injection, he informed her that she was to receive no more. She began the desperate search for another physician, and finally found one approximately fifteen miles from her home.

The treatment continued to be successful for another year, at which time I began to receive the same kind of distressing telephone calls that had characterized her earlier trauma. She lost an incredible forty pounds in a few weeks and cried for hours at a time. Her heart raced and palpitated, and she was beset by great weakness and trembling. One desperate call to her physician brought the comment, "It sounds like nerves to me." He prescribed tranquilizers, which made her wildly nervous, as before. Another physician spent a half hour explaining the dangers of estrogen. Finally, she was admitted to a hospital where she underwent scores of diagnostic tests. Her physicians put her through the customary upper and lower gastrointestinal series, glucose tolerance tests and many other diagnostic procedures. But no certain disorder could be identified. Other physicians administered different tests, though nothing definitive was found.

It was clear to me that my mother's primary problem was physical in origin. She and my father had visited our home in California immediately before the onset of these symptoms, and she had been happy and relaxed. Then suddenly, without undue environmental stress, she had begun to decline. I made a long distance call to another physician-friend in Kansas City. I asked him if he felt her problem could again be hormonal, since the symptoms were so similar to the experience thirteen years earlier. He denied the possibility. "Frankly," he said, "I believe estrogen shots are a kind of placebo: they work simply because a woman *thinks* they're going to help. I don't believe they really do very much of anything."

Still, the calls for help came, sometimes two or three times a week. My mother was often crying when she phoned, saying she had neither slept nor eaten in twenty-four hours. Finally, I picked up the telephone and called the Chief of Obstetrics and Gynecology at USC School of Medicine, where I also serve on the faculty. I described her recurrence of symptoms to him, and asked if it sounded hormonal, once more. He answered in the affirmative and gave me the name of a knowledgeable gynecologist at the University of Kansas. I immediately relayed the information to my mother.

To make a long story a bit shorter, the mystery was solved two days later. Through the course of twelve years of injections every week, my mother had accumulated scar tissue in the hip where she received the additional estrogen. Though she continued to get a shot every seven days, she was absorbing practically none of the hormone itself. Her physicians had ruled out the need for estrogen because of the weekly injections, but in reality, she was in a state of severe deprival once more. We are indebted to the man who recognized her plight and rectified the problem with a regular dosage of oral estrogen.

At the time of my mother's initial difficulties in 1959-1960, I was a young graduate student at USC. Though unintentionally, she was giving me a valuable lesson in problems associated with the female climacteric (hormonal readjustment during menopause). I was to need that introduction. Since that time I have kept abreast of the professional literature on this subject and have seen many women who were suffering from the same undetected disorder. They are referred to my office for treatment of emotional distress, yet within minutes the same pattern of hormonal symptoms begins to unfold. Several times I have guessed the disorder correctly even before the woman had said a word, simply by the characteristic look on her face.

I think it would be helpful to list the symptoms which are often associated with the female climacteric. First, however, I must caution the reader to understand that other physical and emotional problems can occasionally produce the same or similar difficulties. Nor should estrogen therapy be seen as a "miracle drug" for all of the genuine emotional distresses of the middle age years. However, for the reader who has a mother or an aunt with this pattern, or is herself suffering from the symptoms which follow, I would strongly recommend that she consult a gynecologist who is associated with a medical school or one who is on the staff of a major hospital in the area. Approximately twenty-two specific ailments can be triggered by estrogen deprival, although few women experience them all. (Though this list was accumulated from my own observations and experience, its accuracy is verified in a recording produced for professionals by Ayerst Laboratories, featuring the voice of Dr. Herbert Kupperman, professor of Obstetrics and Gynecology, New York University. These writings have also been reviewed by Dr. David Hernandez.)

Emotional Symptoms

1. Extreme depression, perhaps lasting for months without relief.
2. Extremely low self-esteem, bringing feelings of utter worthlessness and disinterest in living.
3. Extremely low frustration tolerance, giving rise to outbursts of temper and emotional ventilation.
4. Inappropriate emotional responses, producing tears when things are not sad and depression during relatively good times.
5. Low tolerance to noise. Even the sound of a radio or the normal responses of children can be extremely irritating. Ringing in the ears is also common.
6. Great needs for proof of love are demanded, and in their absence, suspicion of a rival may be hurled at the husband.
7. Interferences with sleep patterns.
8. Inability to concentrate and difficulty in remembering.

Physical Symptoms:

1. Gastrointestinal disorders, interfering with digestion and appetite.
2. "Hot flashes" which burn in various parts of the body for a few seconds.
3. Vertigo (dizziness).
4. Constipation.
5. Trembling.
6. Hands and feet tingle and "go to sleep."
7. Dryness of the skin, especially in specific patches in various places, and loss of elasticity.
8. Dryness of the mucus membranes, especially in the vagina, making intercourse painful or impossible.
9. Greatly reduced libido (sexual desire).
10. Pain in various joints of the body, shifting from place to place (neuralgias, myalgias and arthralgias).
11. Tachycardia (accelerated or racing heartbeat) and palpitation.
12. Headaches.
13. Dark, gloomy circles around the eyes. This is the symptom which I have found most useful in preliminary diagnosis.
14. Loss of weight.

For the besieged woman who staggers into her physician's office with most of these symptoms, her condition has facetiously been called "The falling hand syndrome." She points to her left eyebrow and says, "Oh! My head has been splitting, and my ears have this funny ringing, and my breasts hurt and oh! My stomach is killing me; and I've got this pain in my lower back, and my buttocks hurt and my knee is quivering." Truly, her hand trembles inch by inch from the top of her crown to the bottom of her aching feet. A physician told me recently that his nurse was attempting to obtain a medical history from such a woman who answered affirmatively to every possible disorder. Whatever disease or problem she mentioned, the patient professed to have had it. Finally in exasperation, the nurse asked if her teeth itched, just to see what the patient would say. The woman frowned for a moment, then ran her tongue over her front teeth and said, "Come to think of it, they sure do!" A menopausal woman such as this is likely to think *everything* has gone wrong.

It is my opinion that many members of the medical profession (particularly those outside the specialty of gynecology) are grossly uninformed on the relationship between estrogen levels and emotional stability in women.

Gerald M. Knox, writing in *Better Homes and Gardens,* quotes numerous medical authorities in his article entitled "When the Blues Really Get You Down." In this publication he stated, "Doctors formerly contended that women in their 40s were susceptible to a form of depression called 'involutional melancholia,' presumably brought on when menopause altered the hormonal flow. Most now doubt its existence. They say the old diagnosis merely represented male bias."[1] Anyone who has ever dealt with a woman in a state of severe estrogen deprival will instantly recognize the fallacy of Knox's statement. Male bias, indeed!

Physical dependence on estrogen for some women has far reaching psychological implications, and failure to recognize this fact can be devastating to a menopausal patient.

I was consulted by a forty-year-old woman who came to me in utter desperation. She was haggard and drawn, and wept as she spoke. Several years before she had undergone a thyroidectomy (surgical removal of the thyroid gland) and an oophorectomy (removal of her reproductive organs). These operations deprived her of the important hormones thyroxin and estrogen, yet her surgeon failed to prescribe for their replacement. As could be expected, she began to deteriorate emotionally. She fell into deep depression and cried for hours at a time. Her husband and children were sympathetic but had no idea how to help her. The family felt it was socially unacceptable to seek psychiatric consultation, so she had no choice but to pull into their most remote bedroom and close the door. This unfortunate woman remained behind that door for more than two years, with her family bringing her food and drink during the day. When she finally came to me, I immediately referred her to a physician whom I knew to be knowledgeable in this area. She wrote me an exuberant letter one month later, saying that life had opened up to her for the first time in three years. My experiences with this woman and similar patients has given me an intolerance for physicians who don't "believe" in hormonal therapy even when it is so obviously needed. I am convinced that there are women confined in hospitals for the emotionally disturbed today who are actually suffering from an easily resolved hormonal deprivation.

Before leaving this issue, let me make one more point which may be even more controversial. Estrogen levels are typically measured by a physician during a pelvic examination. In other words, the amount of estrogen in a woman's body is estimated from a vaginal specimen. However, the emotional consequences of estrogen deprival obviously do not occur in the vagina, but somewhere within the brain of a woman. It is entirely possible for a laboratory result to show a "normal" level of estrogen in the vagina of a particular woman, yet she can experience an hormonal deficit in her brain where it is impossible to assess it biochemically. Therefore, many gynecologists now treat the emotional *symptoms,* whether or not the laboratory tests reveal a deficiency. With the exception of a few relatively rare complications (blood clotting problems, primarily) estrogen does not seem to be toxic and can be administered safely and judiciously to those who *appear* to need it. Furthermore, I have seen a dozen or more women who were in a state of hormonal imbalance, although they were receiving *oral* estrogen. The intestine is not a perfect organ, and it fails to assimilate some of the substances which pass through it. Therefore, not everything swallowed is guaranteed to reach the blood stream, which has accounted for menopausal agony in some women who were technically under treatment to prevent it.

Now, having considered depression associated with estrogen deprivation during menopause, let's discuss the emotional problems common to younger women during the menstrual cycle, itself. First, I would like to stress a fact understood by very few women: self-esteem is directly related to estrogen levels; hence, it fluctuates predictably through the twenty-eight-day cycle. The graph which appears below has the same basic shape as the one presented in the last chapter, though its meaning is very different.[2]

NORMAL HORMONE LEVELS AND MOOD. In the normal menstrual cycle, estrogen peaks at midcycle (ovulation). Both estrogen and progesterone circulate during the second half of the cycle, falling off rapidly just prior to menstruation. Moods change with the fluctuating hormone levels: women feel the greatest self-esteem, and the least anxiety and hostility, at midcycle.

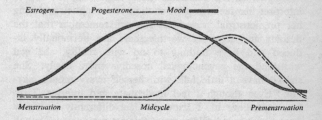

Estrogen——— Progesterone——— Mood ▬▬▬

Menstruation   Midcycle   Premenstruation

Notice that estrogen levels are at their lowest point during menstruation at the left of the graph, as is the general "mood." The production of estrogen increases day by day until it peaks near the time of ovulation at midcycle. That midpoint also happens to be the time of greatest emotional optimism and self-confidence. Then another hormone, progesterone, is produced during the second half of the cycle, bringing with it increasing tension, anxiety, and aggressiveness. Finally, the two hormones decrease during the premenstrual period, reducing the mood to its lowest point again. This regular fluctuation in emotions has been documented repeatedly by various researchers. For example, "Alec Coppen and Neil Kessel studied 465 women and found that they were far more depressed and irritable before menstruation than at midcycle. This was true for neurotic, psychotic and normal women alike. Similarly, Natalie Sharness found the premenstrual phase associated with feelings of helplessness, anxiety, hostility and yearning for love. At menstruation, this tension and irritability eased, but depression often accompanied the relief, and lingered until estrogen increased."[3]

The information provided above can be invaluable to a woman who wants to understand her own body and its impact on her emotions. Most important, she should interpret her feelings with caution and skepticism during her premenstrual period. If she can remember that the despair and sense of worthlessness are hormonally induced and have nothing to do with reality, she can withstand the psychological nosedive more easily. She should have a little talk with herself every month, saying: "Even though I feel inadequate and inferior, I refuse to believe it. I know I'll feel differently in a few days and it is ridiculous to let this get me down. Though the sky looks dark, I am seeing it through a distorted perception. My real problem is physical, not emotional, and it will soon improve!"

Women certainly wish their husbands understood these physiological factors which play such an important role in the female body. Having never had a period, however, it is difficult for a man to comprehend the bloated, sluggish feeling which motivates his wife's snappy remarks and irritability during the premenstrual period. It would be extremely helpful if a husband would learn to anticipate his wife's menstrual period, recognizing the emotional changes which will probably accompany it. Of particular importance will be a need for affection and tenderness during this time, even though she may be rather unlovable for three or four days. He should also avoid discussions of financial problems or other earth-shaking topics until the internal storm has passed, and keep the home atmosphere as tranquil as possible. If his wife seems to be sinking into despair, he should give her the speech described for self-interpretation in the previous paragraph. In summary, the "yearning for love" described by Natalie Sharness can only be satisfied by a sympathetic and knowledgeable husband who cares enough to support his wife during the periodic pressures within.

Author's additional note:
Since this book was first published in 1975, several clinical researchers have observed an apparent link between estrogen therapy and cancer of the uterus. However, this and other potential side effects of hormone replacement therapy remain controversial issues in medical circles and are being debated vigorously from both points of view. Further investigations are currently in progress. It is advised that women with menopausal symptoms seek and accept the counsel of their physicians.

James Dobson, November 1976

Questions and Answers

Question: Is there a "male menopause" comparable to what you described for women?

Answer: This is another question with strong cultural overtones which have clouded the truth. Some members of the feminist movement apparently fear that female menopause will be used as an excuse to withhold positions of leadership from middle-aged women. Therefore, they stress the existence of a comparable "male menopause." While men do experience a climacteric which can be called menopausal, it is very different in origin and impact from that experienced by women. For men, the changes are not so related to hormonal alterations but are more psychological in nature. It is difficult for a man to face the fact that he will never reach the occupational goals that he set for himself . . . that his youth is rapidly vanishing . . . that he will soon be unattractive to the opposite sex . . . that his earlier dreams of glory and power will never be realized. Some men who have achieved less than they hoped are devastated by the realization that life is slipping away from them. This, primarily, is the male menopause. Some individuals respond to it by seeking an affair with a young girl to prove their continued virility; others work harder and longer to overcome the inevitable; others become alcoholics; others enter into dramatic periods of depression. But even when the emotional impact is extreme, it is usually motivated from the man's evaluation of his outside world. These same influences agitate a woman, but she has an additional hormonal turmoil undermining her security from within. Other things being equal, the feminine variety is more difficult to endure, particularly if it remains untreated.

Question: Why do some women make it through menopause without the need for exogenous estrogen?

Answer: I don't think anyone can answer that question, because no one knows for sure what estrogen does to the feminine neurological apparatus. Perhaps the ovaries or the adrenal glands emit enough estrogen to satisfy the needs of a less vulnerable individual. At this point, little is known about the chemistry of the brain and the substances which are necessary for its proper functioning. The guide in treatment then, is the clinical signs and symptoms which the physician observes.

Incidentally, the human female is the only member of the animal kingdom who outlives her reproductive capacity. All others die when their ability to bear young has ended. (Does that help your self-esteem?) The twenty or thirty additional years typically granted to a woman can be the most meaningful and fulfilling in life, if her body is maintained and the proper attitudes are fostered.

Question: Are premenstrual periods similar to menopause in emotional characteristics?

Answer: In the sense that estrogen levels are reduced during both phases, yes. Since self-esteem is apparently related to estrogen, for example, a woman's feelings of inferiority are evident both premenstrually and during menopause. Though I have no evidence to support this hypothesis, I suspect that women who experience severe emotional fluctuations during their periods will probably be most in need of hormonal therapy during later menopause. In other words, the vulnerability to estrogen is demonstrated early in life and confirmed during the middle-age years.

Question: Since "the pill" is actually composed of estrogen, do women who take it fluctuate emotionally as you have described?

Answer: It depends on the kind of pill prescribed. If estrogen and progestin (synthetic progesterone) are given *simultaneously* for twenty days and then ceased, the mood remains at a moderately low level and is characterized by anxiety throughout the month. However, if estrogen is given for fifteen days and estrogen-progestin for five, the mood fluctuation is very similar to the normal non-pill cycle. Your physician can provide more information as to your particular pill and its emotional reverberations.

Question: When my wife is suffering from premenstrual tension, she not only becomes irritable and short-tempered, but she seems to become even more angry when I try to tell her everything will be all right and that it isn't as bad as it seems. How do you explain that?

Answer: You are observing the same lesson that I had to learn in my earlier counseling experience. I remember one patient in particular who used to call me or visit my office every twenty-eight days without exception. She was always tremendously depressed and agitated, but she never seemed to realize that her despair was related to her hormonal calendar. I would explain to her that she wasn't really so bad off, and things would be much better in a few days. To my surprise, however, these attempts to console her only caused greater frustration and made her try to prove to me how terrible things were in her life. She almost seemed insulted by my emphasis on the positive. After thinking about her "plight" for a while, I realized the mistake I was making in handling her case. By tossing out easy, glib answers to her problems, I was depriving her of the one thing she most needed from me. She had not come to me for "answers," but for the assurance that one other human being on earth understood what she was going through. She wanted to know that I comprehended how tough it was, but my pacifying remarks only forced her to prove that she was suffering worse than I thought.

After that, when this woman came to see me, I offered her empathy and understanding, helping her express the frustrations bottled up within. On some occasions I provided nothing more than an accepting atmosphere in which she could ventilate. She would weep for forty or fifty minutes, telling me that there was no hope at all, and then blow her nose and sniff and say, "Thank you for your help. I feel so much better and I don't know what I would have done without you to talk to today." All I had done was let her know I understood. That was enough.

I suspect that your wife wants the same reassurance. There are times when we could *all* use a dose of that commodity.

CHAPTER NINE

Problems
with the Children

The eighth most common source of depression among the women completing our questionnaire was *Problems with the Children*. Please keep in mind that the youthful age of the individuals surveyed undoubtedly influenced the lower ranking of this category of difficulties. If the majority of respondents had been the mothers of adolescents instead, this item might have zoomed to the top of the hit parade of problems.

I have written two books specifically for parents and teachers (*Dare to Discipline* and *Hide or Seek*) both relating to the content of this chapter. Thousands more have been written on the same topic by other authors. Since it is impossible to present an encyclopedic overview of the innumerable problems which confront our children, I will limit discussion to a few aspects of parenthood which are particularly relevant to the role of fatherhood.

The August 1974 issue of *Scientific American* included an important article entitled, "The Origins of Alienation," by Urie Bronfenbrenner. Dr. Bronfenbrenner is, in my opinion, the foremost authority on child development in America today, and his views should be considered carefully. In his article, Dr. Bronfenbrenner discussed the deteriorating status of the American family and the forces which are weakening its cohesiveness. More specifically, he is concerned about the circumstances which are seriously undermining the parental role and depriving children of the leadership and love they must have for survival.

One of those circumstances is widely known as the "rat-race" (which I discussed within the chapter on Fatigue and Time Pressure). Dr. Bronfenbrenner described the problem this way, "The demands of a job that claim meal times, evenings and weekends as well as days; the trips and moves necessary to get ahead or simply to hold one's own; the increasing time spent commuting, entertaining, going out, meeting social and community obligations . . . all of these produce a situation in which a child often spends more time with a passive babysitter than with a participating parent."[1]

According to Dr. Bronfenbrenner, this rat race is particularly incompatible with fatherly responsibilities, as illustrated by a recent investigation which yielded startling results. A team of researchers wanted to learn how much time middle-class fathers spend playing and interacting with their small children. First, they asked a group of fathers to estimate the time spent with their one-year-old youngsters each day, and received an average reply of fifteen to twenty minutes. To verify these claims, the investigators attached microphones to the shirts of small children for the purpose of recording actual parental verbalization. The results of this study are shocking: The average amount of time spent by these middle-class fathers with their small children was thirty-seven seconds per day! Their direct interaction was limited to 2.7 encounters daily, lasting ten to fifteen seconds each! That, so it seems, represents the contribution of fatherhood for millions of America's children.

Now, I'm certain that many fathers are not represented

by the study I've quoted, but who can deny that the rapid pace of our lives interferes with meaningful family relationships? Fathers are working long hours and moonlighting to try to maintain a decent standard of living. When they do come home they are exhausted and have little energy left to invest in their loved ones. And so it is that many wives have the *full* responsibility for the care of their children. Raising kids is a pretty awesome task, even when the job is handled by a team of two, as intended. It can be downright terrifying when approached as a solitary endeavor. In the first place, parenthood is a guilty affair. No matter how hard one tries, it is impossible to discharge the responsibility perfectly. Children are maddeningly complicated, and *no one* has all the answers to the myriad of problems that can arise. Furthermore, both the masculine and feminine personalities are needed in modeling of roles for children. Each gender makes its own contribution to the development of little minds, and a mother knows she is not equipped to play both parts. There's no doubt about it, raising children as a "single parent" (whether married or not) is the loneliest job in the world!

How are women coping with this "solitude of the seventies"? Not too well, it would appear. For one thing, the frustrations I have described have apparently turned parenthood into a distasteful responsibility to be avoided. A recent issue of *Esquire* magazine featured a series of articles entitled, "Does America Suddenly Hate Its Kids?" The theme of the publication is interesting to me, for it deals with a social trend that I have also observed. We have come through a period of extreme child-centeredness, where the entire world revolved around the next generation. Mothers in the fifties and early sixties devoted every ounce of their energy to raising the best educated, best mannered, best fed, best clothed and best medicated kids on the block. But the pendulum has swept back, as pendulums do, to the other side of the continuum. Now, said *Esquire,* many American women have apparently decided that raising children is an enormous interference and sacrifice. How can a woman do her own thing when she is changing diapers and handling the rest of the routine chores on Nursery Hill? As a result of this radical shift in values and attitudes, our little ones are often resented and rejected—or even hated. I have been witnessing evidence of the same disenchantment with parenthood in my professional experience. One young mother told me in a counseling session, "My kids hang around my ankles and try to take all my time, but I kick 'em off. I tell them, 'You're not going to wreck my life!' "

A gruesome set of statistics seems to validate the hypothesis proposed by *Esquire* magazine. The killing of children under one year of age has been increasing year by year, rising 51 percent from 1957 to 1970. Furthermore, there are now between two and four million cases per year of "battered children" who have been brutally beaten and burned and drowned by the adults in their lives. (One mother cut out her child's eyes with a razor blade!) More than 90 percent of these tragic incidents occur in the children's own homes, which should be a place of safety and love. And as might be expected, the most severe injuries were inflicted by mothers in single-parent homes, a fact which reflects the frustration and desperation experienced by some young mothers today.

One of the cornerstone philosophies of the feminist movement asserts that it is *impossible* for a woman to be fulfilled while staying home and raising children. This view must be meeting widespread approval. As stated earlier, almost half the mothers in this nation are employed outside the home. While this percentage is much higher than a few years ago, the greatest increase is being seen with the mothers of preschool children. *One in every three mothers with children under six is employed today*. That statistic distresses me more than I can find words to express. Who is at home to care for those impressionable babies? Who is taking Mom's place? Fifty years ago, half the households had at least one adult besides the parents living with the family. Now the figure is only 4 percent. There is *no* one else at home.

Modern women are struggling to convince themselves that state-sponsored child-care centers offer a convenient substitute for the traditional family concept. It will not work! It hasn't succeeded in the countries where it has been tried. Once more I find myself in agreement with Dr. Bronfenbrenner who wrote: ". . . with the withdrawal of the social supports for the family to which I alluded above, the position of women and mothers has become more and more isolated. With the breakdown of the community, the neighborhood and the extended family, an increasing responsibility for the care and upbringing of children has fallen on the young mother. *Under these circumstances, it is not surprising that many young women in America are in revolt. I understand and share their sense of rage, but I fear the consequences of some of the solutions they advocate, which will have the effect of isolating children still further from the kind of care and attention they need.*"[2]

Children *cannot* raise themselves properly. This fact was illustrated again in a recent conversation with a research psychologist who visited my office. He had been studying the early childhoods of inmates at a state prison in Arizona. He and his associates were seeking to discover the common characteristics which the prisoners shared, hoping to unlock the causes for their antisocial behavior. It was initially assumed that poverty would be the common thread, but their findings contradicted this expectation. The inmates came from all socioeconomic levels of society, though most of them attempted to excuse their crimes by professing to have been poor. Instead, the researchers discovered one fundamental characteristic shared by the men: an absence of adult contact in their early home lives. As children, they spent most of their time in the company of their peers . . . or altogether alone. Such was the childhood of Lee Harvey Oswald, Charles Manson, and many other perpetrators of violent crimes later in life. The conclusion is inescapable: there is no substitute for loving parental leadership in the early development of children.

May I make an appeal to husbands and fathers in concluding this brief discussion? I will speak bluntly, though I don't intend to offend or alienate my masculine readers. If you want your wife to accept the responsibility of motherhood and all that it implies, then you must provide her with your support and involvement. You must let her talk to you when she has had a difficult day with the children, offering suggestions and alternative approaches; you must help her discipline and train and guide; you must meet her emotional and romantic needs which accumulate in your absence; you must understand her requirement to get away from her small children at least once a week; and most important, you must reserve some of your time for your family. It is easy for a man to invest six or seven days a week in his job, because he often loves what he does. His ego-needs are met through his occupation, which encourages him to work fourteen hours a day. When this occurs, however, it sets off a chain reaction of consequences which is enormously disruptive to those who depend on him.

A recent book for families is based on the thesis that a mother sets the dominant tone for her entire household. The ultimate happiness of every member of the family, the author says, is dependent on how well she does her job and the warmth she exudes. While I don't minimize the vital role played by a mother, I believe a successful family *begins* not with her but with her husband. If a woman is to have the contentment and self-satisfaction necessary to produce a successful family, she needs the constant support and respect of the man she loves.

Questions and Answers

Question: You have spoken out strongly against the "child-care center" concept. Do you oppose the idea of nursery or preschool education, as well? What is the difference between the two?

Answer: Your question is an important one and it permits me to clarify my concern on this matter. The concept of nursery school or preschool is very different from the child-care center. Nursery school programs can be of great benefit to a child, particularly in the area of learning socialization skills. A youngster can be taught to share toys, follow instructions, sit in a group, and be offered some rudimentary educational instruction. My own son attends such a program near our home, and has profited from the experience. There are three main differences between this kind of facility, which I see as productive, and the child-care center, which I view as destructive. First, the amount of time that a child spends in such a school is an important variable. For the mother who works full-time, her three-year-old may be out of his home forty-five to fifty hours a week (adding Mom's lunch hours and driving time to her usual eight-hour days). I would not want to see a three-year-old in "school" more than three shorter days a week, and hopefully only two. Second, nursery school for the children of mothers who are not employed frees them to be with other adults, enjoy shopping or bowling or some other form of recreation, or, just gives them time to catch up on loose ends. It lightens her load for a brief time and gets her away from the constant supervision of her youngster. A child-care center, on the other hand, is designed to let the mother work—which means she is likely to be exhausted when she picks up her little one. Third, no preschool or nursery school is geared for babies from birth to three, yet the child-care center is. In my opinion, *anything* which substitutes for the arms of a mother in the first three years should be viewed with great suspicion.

I know I'm virtually alone on this issue, but that makes me neither right *nor* wrong. I would not be true to my own conscience if I failed to express these strong beliefs.

Question: Isn't it true that the *quality* of the time a mother spends with her child is more important than the *quantity*?

Answer: That is a widely-quoted proverb which serves to reduce guilt in parents who are rarely at home. While the statement is true (a small amount of meaningful time with children is better than a longer period of less constructive interaction), I have not found it to have much relevance to the "great debate" regarding working wives. Who says that a working mother's evening time with her children is necessarily of greater quality than it would have been if she remained at home all day? Her fatigue would make the opposite more likely. Anyway, why must we choose between these desirable components: let's give our babies both quality *and* quantity.

Question: How do you feel about the mothers of elementary school children being employed outside the home?

Answer: Much less strongly, although I still believe the family life runs more smoothly and effectively when a mother does not work full time. The key factor is to be home when the troops come storming in from school.

Question: Can you recommend a good book for those of us men who would like to do a better job as fathers?

Answer: First, I would suggest that you read *Father Power*, by Henry Biller and Dennis Meredith.[3] It endorses the views I have expressed on the critical importance of fatherhood and offers many suggestions for improving one's performance in that endeavor. Secondly, you might enjoy *How to Father*, by James Fitzhugh Dodson.[4] (Dr. Dodson and I are frequently mistaken for each other. I was introduced as Dr. Dodson during my first appearance on the Dinah Shore Show, and we have both been trying to straighten out the confusion ever since. Please help us spread the word. There are two of us—count them—two distinct individuals.)

Question: What answer do you have for those who say being a mother and a housewife is boring and monotonous?

Answer: They are right—but we should recognize that practically every other occupation is boring, too. How exciting is the work of a telephone operator who plugs and unplugs switchboard connections all day long—or a medical pathologist who examines microscopic slides and bacterial cultures from morning to night—or a dentist who spends his lifetime drilling and filling, drilling and filling—or an attorney who reads dusty books in a secluded library—or an author who writes page after page after page? Few of us enjoy heart-thumping excitement each moment of our professional lives. On a trip to Washington, D.C., last week, my hotel room was located next to the room of a famous cellist, who was in the city to give a classical concert that evening. I could hear him through the walls as he practiced hour after hour. He did not play beautiful symphonic renditions; he repeated scales and runs and exercises, over and over and over. This practice began early in the morning (believe me!) and continued to the time of his concert. As he strolled on stage that evening, I'm sure many individuals in the audience thought to themselves, "What a glamorous life!" Some glamor! I happen to know that he had spent the entire day in his lonely hotel room in the company of his cello. Musical instruments, as you know, are terrible conversationalists. No, I doubt if the job of a housewife and mother is much more boring than most other jobs, particularly if the woman refuses to be isolated from adult contact. But as far as importance of the assignment is concerned, *no* job can compete with the responsibility of shaping and molding a new human being.

May I remind mothers of one more important consideration: you will not always be saddled with the responsibility you now hold. Your children will be with you for a few brief years and the obligations you now shoulder will be nothing more than dim memories. Enjoy every moment of these days—even the difficult times—and indulge yourself in the satisfaction of having done an essential job right!

Question: How do you feel about a man doing his share of the housework and helping with the meals at home?

Answer: My opinion on that subject is not likely to win me great numbers of friends among the women of the world, but I dislike seeing a man work all day at his job and then be *obligated* to confront his wife's responsibility when he comes home (assuming that she has no outside employment of her own). I know women who have browbeaten their puppy-dog husbands into cooking and washing dishes every night of the year. This is not the commitment I was describing in the preceding chapter, although there are times when a loving husband will choose to bail out his overworked wife. Personally, I balk when I think my wife is demanding that I go beyond the call of duty; I like to help her on a *voluntary* basis, and often do so.

I would not include the management of children in the division of labor described above, because the raising of kids is not a mother's sole responsibility! Boys and girls need their fathers as much as their mothers, and I certainly do not consider the time I spend with my children as a favor to my wife. Each evening that I am home, I oversee their bedtime preparations—brushing the teeth, administering the baths, putting on Ryan's pajamas, saying the prayers, and hauling four to six glasses of water to each little procrastinator. This gives me a few moments exclusively with the children each day and I try to make it a fun time. When Ryan was still in diapers, for example, we played a game with the pins each night. I would "talk to the pins" and tell them not to stick him as they were going through the diapers. "Please don't stick little Ryan," I pled. "He's not really a bad kid. He's not wiggling around at all and I think you should be nice to him." Every now and then when Ryan would squirm and make it difficult to get his diapers on, I would let the point of a pin scrape his skin. He would frown and say, "Those mean ol' pins sticked me, Dad!" I would scold them and warn them about further assaults of that kind. Ryan never seemed to tire of this game and insisted that I "talk to the pins" every night. Children love *routine* games, and these kinds of creative experiences can turn a chore into a time of togetherness—provided you're not too pooped to care.

Question: Is divorce really as destructive to children as we have been led to believe?

Answer: Children are amazingly resilient, and they do manage to "bounce back" from some severe traumas and crises. Much depends, of course, on how much conflict they witness and how wisely the parent in custody is able to handle the problems. Generally speaking, however, divorce is extremely difficult for the children involved. The comedian Jonathan Winters verified this fact when he appeared as the guest on a television interview program. The host asked Mr. Winters to describe his early childhood, and he became unusually serious as he spoke. He described the disintegration of his family when Jonathan was seven years old, and how deeply he was hurt by the divorce. He said the other children would tease and laugh at him because he didn't have a father, and he reacted with anger. He would fight his tormentors and shake his fist in their faces, but when they were not looking he would go off behind a tree or building and cry. Mr. Winters indicated that he later learned to laugh his way out of trouble, but admitted that all of his adult humor is a response to sorrow.

Children of broken homes usually learn to cope with

their situation, one way or another, but the emotional impact will never be completely forgotten.

Question: Can you give some specific guidelines which will help me raise my newborn son during the next two or three years? I know there are many books on this subject, but I would like to learn where the general target lies.

Answer: Researchers at the Harvard University Laboratory of Human Development have drawn up a list of guidelines which may be helpful to you. They have delineated nine "do's" and thirteen "don'ts," which were quoted in *Today's Health,* as follows:

According to the researchers, the child should be given relatively free access, where possible, within the home. This freedom provides him with maximum opportunity to exercise his curiosity and explore his world. But this world should be safety-proofed: Good books and expensive vases should be placed on high shelves, leaving old magazines and suitable playthings in their place. Low kitchen cabinets can be emptied of dangerous or breakable objects.

The staff also recommends that the mother be available to the child during at least half of his waking hours. This does not mean that she has to hover over him, but that she is nearby to provide needed attention, support, or assistance.

When the child wants the mother's attention, she should:

1. Respond promptly and favorably as often as possible.
2. Make some effort to understand what the child is trying to do.
3. Set limits—do not give in to unreasonable requests.
4. Provide encouragement, enthusiasm, and assistance whenever suitable.
5. Talk to the child as often as possible.

6. Use words he understands—and also add new words.

7. Use words to provide a related idea. If the child shows you a ball, ask him to "Throw the ball" to you.

8. Take only as much time as is needed in the situation, even if it's only a few seconds.

9. Encourage "pretend" activities.

There are other times, too, when the mother will want to initiate the interaction with the child. If the child is bored, she should provide things for him to do. When he misbehaves, the mother must discipline him firmly and consistently. If he wants to try something new that might be unsafe, such as climbing the stairs, the mother should supervise rather than stop him from doing it.

On the basis of their observations, the staff also drew up a list of practices for mothers to avoid:

1. Don't cage the child or confine him regularly for long periods.

2. Don't allow him to concentrate his energies on you to the point where he spends most of his time following you around or staying near you, especially in his second year of life.

3. Don't ignore your child's attention-getting devices to the point where he throws a tantrum to gain your interest.

4. Don't worry that your baby won't love you if you say "no" from time to time.

5. Don't try to win all the arguments with a child —especially from the middle of the second year when he may start becoming negative.

6. Don't try to prevent him from cluttering the house; it's an inevitable sign of a healthy, curious baby.

7. Don't be overprotective.

8. Don't overpower him; let him do what he wants to do as often as is safe.

9. Don't take a full-time job or otherwise make yourself largely unavailable to the child during this period of his life.

10. Don't bore your child if you can avoid it.

11. Don't worry about when he learns to read, count numbers, or say the alphabet. Don't even worry if he's slow to talk, as long as he seems to understand more and more language as he grows.

12. Don't try to force toilet training. By the time he's two or over, it will be easy.

13. Don't hover over or spoil your child—he may think the whole world was made just for him.[5]

CHAPTER TEN

A Brief Visit
with Father Time

Note: The ninth most common source of depression for the study group was generated by In-law Problems. This matter will be discussed briefly in the final chapter. First I want to discuss number ten: aging.

Several months ago, I was driving my car near our home with my son and daughter and Ryan's three-year-old friend, Kevin. As we turned a corner we drove past a very old man who was so bent and crippled that he could hardly walk. We talked about how the man must feel, and then I told the kids that they would someday grow old, too. That bit of news was particularly shocking to Kevin, and he refused to accept it.

"I'm not going to get old!" he said, as though insulted by my prediction.

"Yes, you are, Kevin," I said, "all of us will grow old if we live that long. It happens to everyone."

His eyes grew big and he protested again, "But it won't happen to me!"

I again assured him that none can escape.

Kevin sat in silence for fifteen or twenty seconds, and

then he said with a note of panic in his voice, "But! But! But I don't want to grow old. I want to stay fresh and good."

I said, "I know, Kevin! How well I know!"

The inability to stay "fresh and good" produced the tenth most common source of depression for the women who completed our questionnaire. Once again, the young age of the individuals surveyed certainly influenced the relatively low ranking of this item. I'm sure that it will move up on the scale in the next few years. There is something distressing about watching yourself disintegrate day by day, especially after it dawns on you that life itself is a fatal disease. None of us is going to get out of it alive!

I heard a story about three elderly people who were sitting in rocking chairs on the front porch of their rest home. One said to the others, "You know, I don't hear so well anymore and I thought it would bother me more than it does. But there isn't much that I want to hear, anyway."

The second woman said, "Yes, I've found the same thing with my eyes. Everything looks blurred and cloudy now, but I don't care. I saw just about everything that I wanted to see when I was younger."

The third lady thought for a moment and then said, "Well, I don't know about that. I sort of miss my mind . . ."

We can laugh together about those experiences which are inevitable for all of life's survivors. (It happens so quickly, too: about the time your face clears up, your mind gets fuzzy!) But I have a special empathy for those who are locked in the loneliness and isolation of old age. Physiologically, there is a predictable pattern which is typical of the aging process, beginning *with* the malfunction of the sensory apparatus. At first, the ability to see, hear, feel, taste, and smell all begin to deteriorate. Then the cardio-vascular system becomes less efficient and the muscles and joints refuse to operate properly. This is a difficult stage in life because the mind is then a captive inside a body that no longer serves it. Finally, as the last phase in the decline of a normal but aging body, the neurones begin to break in the brain and senility robs the mind of its capacity to reason.

Oliver Wendell Holmes has offered the best analysis of old age in a timeless poem that I have enjoyed since boyhood. This piece describes an elderly man who outlived all of his friends and loved ones, and now clings to an old forsaken bough as *The Last Leaf on the Tree*:

I saw him once before,
As he passed by the door,
   And again
The pavement stones resound,
As he totters o'er the ground
   With his cane.

They say that in his prime,
Ere the pruning-knife of Time
   Cut him down,
Not a better man was found
By the Crier on his round
   Through the town.

But now he walks the streets,
And he looks at all he meets
   Sad and wan,
And he shakes his feeble head,
That it seems as if he said,
   "They are gone."

The mossy marbles rest
On the lips that he has prest
   In their bloom,
And the names he loved to hear
Have been carved for many a year
   On the tomb.

My grandmamma has said—
Poor old lady, she is dead
   Long ago—
That he had a Roman nose,
And his cheek was like a rose
   In the snow;

But now his nose is thin,
And it rests upon his chin
   Like a staff,
And a crook is in his back,
And a melancholy crack
   In his laugh.

I know it is a sin
For me to sit and grin
   At him here;
But the old three-cornered hat,
And the breeches, and all that,
   Are so queer!

And if I should live to be
The last leaf upon the tree
   In the spring,
Let them smile as I do now,
At the old forsaken bough
   Where I cling.

This weird old man is not the only leaf that clings to a forsaken bough. There are other trees in other places. I will not soon forget a television program aired in Los Angeles which was devoted to the topic of aging. It was one of those unusual documentaries which burns its way into the viewer's memory forever. The subject for the half-hour program was an eighty-eight-year-old woman named Elizabeth Holt Hartford. She lived in a tiny room of a decrepit hotel in the slum section of Los Angeles. The film crews for the station selected Miss Hartford to dramatize the plight of the poverty-stricken, sick old people who populate the central part of the city. Though she was wrinkled and bowed by time, Miss Hartford was remarkably lucid and eloquent. Her message still rings in my ears, and it sounded like this: "You see me as an ancient old woman, but I want to tell you something. This is *me* inside here. I haven't changed; I'm just stuck within this broken old body and I can't get out. It hurts me and it won't move right and it gets tired whenever I try to do anything. But the real me is not what you see. I am a prisoner within this decaying body!"

Elizabeth Holt Hartford is a prisoner no longer. She died a few months later, and the ashes from her cremated body were scattered among some rose bushes near her shoddy hotel.

I must share a personal conviction with each of you at this point. Aside from the anticipation of eternal life on the other side of the grave, old age offers few compensations and consolations. It is often a rugged experience, fraught with loneliness, sickness, poverty and low self-esteem. To pretend otherwise is to deny the reality which exists behind the doors of any home for the elderly. Death never seems to arrive at the right time; it comes either too early or too late. However, for those fortunate Christians who rest in the assurance that a new and better world awaits them beyond the grave, the gloom and pessimism give way to expectation and hope. The final heartbeat for them is *NOT* the end—it is the grand beginning. I intend to be one of those confident old people, if I survive to that time.

My father has always had an enormous influence on me, not only throughout my childhood, but during my adult years as well. He told me recently that eternal life for him was not a matter of great value when he was younger. He had enjoyed his youth, and the thought of an existence beyond the grave was like a pearl that was crusted over with scales and grime. The beauty of the pearl was assumed but not apparent or realized. But as he grew older and began to experience some of the inconveniences of aging, including a serious heart attack and assorted aches and pains, the encrustations fell from the pearl of eternal life, one by one. Now it shines brilliantly, more prized than any other possession in my father's grasp.

In conclusion, let's return to the relationship between men and women as it pertains to the process of aging. What does a woman most want from her husband in the fifth, sixth, and seventh decades of her life? She wants and needs the same assurance of love and respect that she desired when she was younger. This is the beauty of committed love—that which is avowed to be a lifelong devotion. A man and woman can face the good and bad times together as friends and allies. By contrast, the youthful advocate of "sexual freedom" and noninvolvement will enter the latter years of life with nothing to remember but a series of exploitations and broken relationships. That short-range philosophy which gets so much publicity today has a predictable dead-end down the road. Committed love is expensive, I admit, but it yields the highest returns on the investment at maturity.

CHAPTER ELEVEN

The Last Word

Winston Churchill once said, "Writing a book is an adventure. To begin with, it is a toy and an amusement. Then it becomes a mistress, then it becomes a master, then it becomes a tyrant. The last phase is that just as you are about to be reconciled to your servitude, you kill the monster and fling him about to the public."

I have progressed through each of Mr. Churchill's stages in the writing of this book, and now stand ready to lay the dead dragon on the nation's bookshelves. There is but one remaining message that I want to convey and it is intended specifically for distaff readers. Our purpose to this point has been to plead the case of wives to their husbands, hopefully expressing some of those needs and frustrations which they often find difficult to verbalize. In this final chapter, however, I want to offer a word of advice directly to women about how to maintain a healthy emotional balance in the face of depressing circumstances.

When I first began driving to my hospital office in 1966, I noticed a nice-looking man who invariably stood at the window of an old apartment house which is located across the street from the doctors' parking lot. Morning after morning this man, whom I would judge to have been in his middle forties, appeared at that same open window as I drove past. He was always there when I went home at the end of the day, as well. I began to wave or smile to the man in the window, and he would return my greeting with a similar gesture. Though it seems unlikely, we developed a friendship in the absence of any personal knowledge of one another, or without a single conversation between us.

My curiosity finally compelled me to get better acquainted with the man behind the smile. One noontime I walked from my office to the building where my congenial friend lived, and climbed a dark stairway to the second floor. I knocked on the door and it was opened by "the man in the window." He introduced himself as Tommy and invited me to come into his two-room apartment. During the next hour he told me his story. He had been a successful executive until devastated by a massive coronary thrombosis about six years earlier. His heart ailments were compounded by emphysema and other physical disorders, which prevented his engaging in any form of work. I also noticed that his right arm was deformed, being much smaller than his left. Tommy, I learned, was rarely able to leave his tiny apartment. He was not married and seemed to have no relatives or close friends. His situation was not unlike being sentenced to virtual solitary confinement in a two-room cell.

The beautiful part of Tommy's story is how he chose to cope with his personal tragedy . . . He had every reason in the world to be depressed and despondent, but he exuded confidence and optimism. He had decided that he would make friends with as many people as possible among those driving to and from their work, and that comprised his entire social life.

I said, "Tommy, what can I do for you? Do you need anything? Can I help in any way?"

He said, "Thank you, sir, and I appreciate your offer. But I'm doing all right. I really don't need anything."

There was not one ounce of self-pity apparent anywhere in our conversation, and he steadfastly refused to let me treat him as an invalid. His only acknowledgement that life was difficult came in response to my question, "Do you ever become discouraged with your situation here?"

Tommy replied, "Well, in the morning when everyone is coming to work, I enjoy greeting the people at the start of a new day. But when they are heading for their homes at night and I'm saying goodbye, I sometimes feel a little blue." That was the only negative statement I ever heard him utter. Tommy had obviously made up his mind to accept life as it was.

For something more than fifteen years, Tommy stood his watch above the noise and traffic of the street, and we remained good friends. I stopped my car beneath his window on January 3 of this year, to greet him after I had been gone for a brief Christmas vacation. Without thinking, I asked him the traditional question which friends exchange following New Year's Eve: "Did you have a good holiday?"

Tommy replied, "It was great."

I later learned that he had spent the entire Christmas season in the solitude of his room, watching the harassed shoppers and commuters below him.

A few weeks later, Tommy failed to appear at his usual place at the window. The second morning he was absent again, and both his shades were drawn. I learned from the parking lot attendant that Tommy had collapsed and died during the previous weekend. My friend was gone. His funeral had already been held, though I doubt if anyone attended it. Now as I drive past the apartment building each morning, I can hear Tommy saying the last words he ever spoke to me, "It was great."

My point in telling you about Tommy is to illustrate

the fact that depression is usually a matter of perspective. Everything depends on how you look at a given situation. I saw a couple win $3,000 cash on the television program "Let's Make a Deal," but they went home literally sick because they barely missed winning a $12,000 automobile. If Monty Hall had met them on the street and handed them $3,000, they would have been overjoyed. But they were dismayed by the knowledge that they could have won more. It was all a matter of perspective.

A small advertisement appeared in *McCall's* magazine for a product which offers to rid women of that dreaded disorder, *stretch marks*. The ad quoted the sad testimony of a young mother who spoke right from her heart: "I've had two children, but I am so unhappy with the stretch marks on my legs, body, and bust. They make me feel ashamed to be seen in a bathing suit or low-cut clothes." It is entirely possible that this young woman is the mother of two healthy children; she may have a good husband who loves her, and judging from her picture, she is still in the bloom of youth and physical vitality. Everything important may be going right for her, yet she is "so unhappy" and feels "ashamed" because she is not perfect. Her problem is one of perspective. She has allowed one tiny flaw to establish her dominant mood. And don't you know it is pleasant for her husband and children to come home to her each evening!

I know life can bite and cut, and I don't mean to sound unsympathetic regarding the circumstances which adversely affect one's mood. But it will help some readers to recognize that we often *permit* routine things to depress us. Let's consider the example of in-law conflict (which ranked as the ninth most common source of depression in the women surveyed). A wife can decide how she will react to an overpossessive or irritating mother-in-law; she can cry and gnash her teeth and let the conflict drill little holes in the lining of her stomach— or she can view it from a less agitated perspective.

Though it sounds a bit silly, my point will be made by imagining that such a woman had loving, respectful, supportive in-laws, but she also had a child in the leukemia ward of our hospital. Let's suppose that by some stroke of magic I could offer her a healthy child if she would also accept a hostile mother-in-law. She would grab the exchange and be forever thankful for the miracle. It is, as I said, simply a matter of perspective—determined entirely by how one looks at a problem.

A very close and respected friend of mine, whom I'll call Martha, has a father who has never revealed any depth of love for her. Though she is now grown and has two children of her own, she continues to hope that he will suddenly become what he has never been. This expectation causes Martha repeated disappointment and frustration. When her infant son failed to survive his first week of life, her insensitive father didn't even come to the funeral. He still shows little interest in Martha or her family—a fact which has caused deep wounds and scars through the years.

After receiving a letter from Martha in which she again mentioned her father's latest insult (he refused to come to her son's wedding), I sent her a few reactions and suggestions. She said she obtained so much help from what I had written that she shared it with three other women experiencing similar frustrations from people who have "failed" them. Finally, she returned a copy of my letter and asked me to include it in a future book of this nature. It appears below.

Martha, I am more convinced every day that a great portion of our adult effort is invested in the quest for that which was *unreachable* in childhood. The more painful the early void, the more we are motivated to fill it later in life. Your dad never met the needs that a father should satisfy in his little girl, and I think you are still hoping he will miraculously become what he has never been. Therefore, he constantly disappoints you—hurts you—rejects you. I think you will be less vulnerable to pain when you accept the fact that he cannot, nor will he ever, provide the love and empathy and interest that he should. It is not easy to insulate yourself in this way. I'm still working to plug a few vacuums from my own tender years. *But it hurts less to expect nothing than to hope in vain.*

I would guess that your dad's own childhood experiences account for his emotional peculiarities, and can perhaps be viewed as his own unique handicap. If he were blind, you would love him despite his lack of vision. In a sense, he is emotionally "blind." He is unable to see your needs. He is unaware of the hurt behind the unpleasant incidents and disagreements— the funeral of your baby, the disinterest in your life, and now Bob's wedding. His handicap makes it *impossible* for him to perceive your feelings and anticipation. If you can accept your father as a man with a permanent handicap—one which was probably caused when *he* was vulnerable—you will shield yourself from the ice pick of rejection.

You didn't ask for this diatribe, and it may not hit your particular target at all. Nevertheless these are the thoughts which occurred to me as I read your letter.

At least *we* are looking forward to the wedding, Martha. Best wishes to John and Bob and the entire Williams enterprise.

Sincerely,

Jim

This letter was of help to Martha, but not because it improved her distressing circumstances. Her father is no more thoughtful and demonstrative today than he was in years past. It is Martha's *perspective* of him that has been changed. She now sees him as a victim of cruel forces in his own childhood which nicked and scarred his young psyche and caused him to insulate his emotions against the outside world. Since receiving this letter, Martha has learned that her father was subjected to some extremely traumatic circumstances during his childhood. (Among other things, his aunt told him unsympathetically that his father had died suddenly and then she reprimanded him severely for crying.) Martha's father is, as I suspected, a man with a handicap.

Some of the women who have read this book are married to men who will never be able to understand the feminine needs I have described. Their emotional structure makes it impossible for them to comprehend the feelings and frustrations of another—particularly those occurring in the opposite sex. These men will not read a book such as this, and would probably resent it if they did. They have never been required to "give," and have no idea how it is done. What, then, is to be the reaction of their wives? What would *you* do if your husband lacked the insight to be what you need him to be?

My advice is that you change that which can be altered, explain that which can be understood, teach that which can be learned, revise that which can be improved, resolve that which can be settled, and negotiate that which is open to compromise. Create the best marriage possible from the raw materials brought by two imperfect human beings with two distinctly unique personalities. *But for all the rough edges which can never be smoothed and the faults which can never be eradicated, try to develop the best possible perspective and determine in your mind to accept reality exactly as it is.* The first principle of mental health is to accept that which cannot be changed. You could easily go to pieces over the adverse circumstances beyond your control, but like my friend Tommy, you can also resolve to withstand them. You can *will* to hang tough, or you can yield to cowardice. Depression is often evidence of emotional surrender.

Someone wrote:

> Life can't give me joy and peace;
>   it's up to me to *will* it.
> Life just gives me time and space;
>   it's up to me to fill it.

Can you accept the fact that your husband will *never* be able to meet all of your needs and aspirations? Seldom does one human being satisfy every longing and hope in the breast of another. Obviously, this coin has two sides: You can't be his perfect woman, either. He is no more equipped to resolve your entire package of emotional needs than you are to become his sexual dream machine every twenty-four hours. Both partners have to settle for human foibles and faults and irritability and fatigue and occasional nighttime "headaches." A good marriage is not one where perfection reigns; it is a relationship where a healthy perspective overlooks a multitude of "unresolvables." Thank goodness my wife, Shirley, has adopted that attitude toward me!

I said in the previous chapter that my father has influenced my values and attitudes more than any other single contributor. This is particularly true in regard to his respect and love for my mother (and hers in return). They have been married for forty-one years, and their commitment to one another is as steady today as it has been through those four decades. It is fitting that I bring this book to a close by quoting the words of my dad— words that he wrote to my mother on the occasion of her fiftieth birthday. The springtime of that year had set him thinking about the brevity of life and the certainty of old age ahead. The poem which follows is entitled, "Your Birthday," and it made my mother cry:

> The whole world's singing now that spring has come
> I saw a robin in the morning sun
> Among the pale-green leaves and bursting buds I
>   heard his talk
> But it is autumn where we walk.

'Tis true for us the summer too is gone
Now whiplashed winds arise and further on
The ice and sleet and cold in grim assault
    to pierce us through
Does fall in springtime frighten you?

Impotent shines the April sun so fair
To melt the wisps of frost within your hair
My dear, I know you feel the threatening gloom
    But I'm with you
And hand in hand we'll face the winter, too.

Isn't that a beautiful expression of love in its richest meaning? My dad has promised to stand shoulder to shoulder with my mother, even when assaulted by whiplashed winds and threatening gloom. His commitment is not based on ephemeral emotions or selfish desires. It is supported by an uncompromising *will*. Don't you see that this "oneness" of spirit is what women seek in their husbands? We human beings can survive the most difficult of circumstances if we are not forced to stand alone. We are social creatures and can no better tolerate emotional solitude than Adam did before Eve was offered as his companion. Women need men, and men need women, and that's the way it has always been.

I'm sure you have noticed how consistently this same theme has appeared in response to *all* the sources of depression in women. We have been examining, I believe, a single problem with ten separate manifestations. Simply stated, the family was designed by God Almighty to have a specific purpose and function: when it operates as intended, the emotional and physical needs of husbands, wives, and children are met in a beautiful relationship of symbiotic love. But when that function is inhibited or destroyed, then every member of the family experiences the discomfort of unmet needs. That is my message. That is what I came to say in this book. When the family conforms to God's blueprint, then self-esteem is available for everyone—which satisfies romantic aspirations—which abolishes loneliness, isolation, and boredom—which contributes to sexual fulfillment—which binds the marriage together in fidelity—which provides security for children—which gives parents a sense of purpose—which contributes to self-esteem once more. The chain has no weak links. It reveals the beauty of God's own creation, as does the rest of his universe. But it can be spoiled, just as mankind has fouled the air and contaminated the water which God designed for us. When the family is polluted through sexual permissiveness, or selfishness, or incredibly busy lives, then disease replaces health and despondency sits on the front doorstep. The American family is sick today, and the widespread depression of which I have written is but a symptom of that malignancy.

What do women most want from their husbands? It is not a bigger home or a better dishwasher or a newer automobile. Rather, it is the assurance that "hand and hand we'll face the best and worst that life has to offer—together."

A Subsequent Note from the Author

I acknowledged within the final chapter of this text that many men would not read a book of this nature and might resent its message if they did. That prediction was written three years ago, and I'm pleased to say that it has not proved to be accurate. Many men have read "What Wives Wish . . ." and their response has been gratifying. Nevertheless, the most frequent question I am asked by wives remains, "How can I get my husband to read your book?"

Until now, I've had no answer to that inquiry. Recently, however, it became apparent that some men will listen to cassette tapes when they will not read the content in written form. Therefore, we have recorded a set of six tapes by the same title as the book. They present the major themes of this text as expressed through my speeches, interviews and radio broadcasts. The final tapes are devoted to a discussion wih Dr. David Hernandez, (the obstetrician and gynecologist mentioned in Chapter Eight), presenting the implications of menstrual and physiological problems and sexual inadequacies.

This album can be obtained at your Christian bookstore, or ordered from the address provided on page 189. It is, I feel, the most important recorded series of my professional life.

Thank you,
James Dobson
April, 1978

Notes

CHAPTER ONE

1. Proverbs 31:23.

CHAPTER THREE

1. Joyce Landorf, *The Fragrance of Beauty* (Wheaton, Il.: Victor Books, 1973).

CHAPTER FOUR

1. James Dobson, *Hide or Seek* (Old Tappan, N.J.: Fleming H. Revell Co., 1974), pp. 53-55. Used by permission.

2. Ibid., pp. 59, 60.

CHAPTER FIVE

1. Judith Viorst, "Just Because I'm Married Does It Mean I'm Going Steady?" *Redbook*, May 1973, p. 62. Reprinted by permission.

CHAPTER SEVEN

1. Paul Popenoe, "Are Women Really Different?" *Family Life*, February 1971, Vol. XXXI, No. 2. Used by permission.

2. From *Cosmopolitan* magazine, June 1974 issue. Quoted by permission.

CHAPTER EIGHT

1. Gerald M. Knox, "When the Blues Really Get You Down," *Better Homes and Gardens*, January 1974, p. 12f. Used by permission.

2. Adapted from *Psychology Today*, February 1972, p. 53. Used by permission.

3. Reprinted from *Psychology Today* Magazine, February 1972. Copyright © 1972. Ziff-Davis Publishing Company. All rights reserved. Used by permission.

CHAPTER NINE

1. Urie Bronfenbrenner, "The Origins of Alienation," *Scientific American*, August 1974, p. 54. Quoted by permission.

2. Ibid., p. 57.

3. Published by David McKay, New York, N.Y. 1975.

4. Published by Nash Publications, Los Angeles, Ca., 1974.

5. Martin Cohen, "A Warning to Conscientious Mothers," *Today's Health*, February 1974. Reprinted by permission.

Other Materials for the Family by Dr. James Dobson

Books:

Dare to Discipline, Tyndale House Publishers, 1970. (Over one million copies of this text have been sold).

Hide or Seek, Self-Esteem for the Child, Fleming H. Revell Publishing Company, 1974.

The Mentally Retarded Child and His Family, Brunner-Mazel Publishers, 1970. (This book was co-edited with Dr. Richard Koch).

The Strong-willed Child, Tyndale House Publishers, 1978.

Preparing for Adolescence, Vision House Publishers, 1978. This book is based on the tapes, described below, and is intended to help the pre-adolescent (and junior high student) cope with the pressures of growing up.

Cassettes:

Discipline: Cradle to College, Vision House Publishers (One Way Library), 1978. This album contains six cassette tapes, based on the concepts discussed in the book by the same name.

Preparing for Adolescence Tapes, Vision House Publishers (One Way Library), 1975. This album contains six cassette tapes, designed to help the pre-teenager prepare for the experience to come. Also available are instructional tapes for parents and a workbook for junior highers.

Kids Need Self-Esteem Too, Vision House Publishers (One Way Library), 1978. This album contains six cassette tapes, and presents the ways parents and teachers can maximize self confidence in children.

What Wives Wish Their Husbands Knew about Women, Vision House Publishers (One Way Library), 1977. This album deals with the basic content of the book by the same name, although it contains speeches, radio interviews and counseling conversations.

Focus on the Family, Word Publishers, 1978. This 12 tape album reflects Dr. Dobson's views on successful family living as related to television viewing, spiritual training of children, marital conflicts, family traditions, etc.

These items are available in local bookstores, or can be ordered by writing Box 952, Temple City, California, 91780. Dr. Dobson can also be contacted through that address, although he regrets that he is unable to respond to requests for personal consultation.